GW00361790

2016
Wilson On Wine
THE WINES TO DRINK THIS YEAR

IRISH TIMES BOOKS

in association with

Santa Rita

Published by: The Irish Times Limited
Editor: Joe Breen
Design & Layout: Angelo McGrath.
Photographer: Marc O'Sullivan
Printed by: Printrun

© John Wilson 2015.
© The Irish Times 2015.
© Marc O' Sullivan (images) 2015

ISBN: 978 0 9070 11460

2016
Wilson On Wine
THE WINES TO DRINK THIS YEAR

Welcome to the second edition of Wilson on Wine. The idea is pretty much the same as last year; these are the best and most interesting wines I have tasted over the last 12 months. Even after all these years, I still get excited by a wine. You come across one that stops you in your tracks; a wine with an astonishing range of flavours that come together to form a perfect whole. Or you could be simply sitting out in the sun, or maybe around the dinner table, talking to friends, when you are served a glass of something fairly simple that seems, at that moment, to be the most perfect drink ever.

Over 90 per cent of the entries in this book are new. That doesn't mean all of last year's wines have suddenly gone off. But we all need to refresh our palates and broaden our horizons. The world of wine moves on as new regions are discovered and old ones regenerate. So keep hold of your 2015 edition of WoW and use it alongside this year's model. As for the 10% that get entries this and last year, they are simply too good to leave out!

My choices are partly influenced by where I travel and what I taste there. This year I include nine wines from Austria, and eight from New Zealand. Austria has been making brilliant white wines for years. Now the reds are catching up. It makes for a thrilling range. We are all familiar with Marlborough Sauvignon. It is one of our most popular wines. But not all taste the same, so this year I have four of my favourites, ranging in price from €8.79 to €33, including a few very different takes on this variety. I list several Pinot Noirs, a variety that is wildly successful in New Zealand and now Australia too. I also include a Romanian Pinot Noir as well as wines from Slovenia, Lebanon, Greece, and England (yes, England!).

In the future I am certain we will drink more wines made from organic or even biodynamic grapes. We will also demand wines made in a less interventionist way with fewer additives. This can only be a good thing. So-called natural wines, made with little or no sulphur dioxide, are a very divisive subject. SO_2 has been used since Roman times to prevent wines from spoiling or oxidising. I have selected a few natural wines that I enjoyed. In addition, this year I note wines made from organically-grown grapes.

As with last year, there are very few supermarket wines. This is not down to any snobbery on my side. I enjoy some of their bottles and believe they have a vital role in the business of wine. However, their ranges tend to be seasonal, featuring once-off parcels. Each multiple engages in a bewildering series of offers, promotions, and special deals. It is impossible to know the real price of a wine.

But I certainly believe that if you are searching for interesting bottles the best place to look is your local off-licence, wine shop, or online specialist retailer. These people tend to deal with smaller, more exciting producers. They can also provide expert help and advice should you need it.

I am grateful for the continued support of Santa Rita, The Irish Times and, of course, you the reader. Without you, this guide would have no purpose. Here's hoping it helps you find something new and exciting to drink in the year ahead. By the way, if you come across a really good bottle of wine, I would love to hear about it. You can contact me at any of the addresses below.

Happy Drinking!

John Wilson on Wine
jwilson@irishtimes.com
Blog www.wilsononwine.ie
Twitter @wilsononwine
Facebook Wilsononwine

IRISH TIMES BOOKS

in association with

THE WINE STYLES

Describing wines is never easy or exact; one person's cherries can be another's plums. I have tried to keep the tasting notes as short as possible and to avoid very florid descriptions. I hope that they will give you a real sense of the wine's taste. I also give a possible food match with each wine, some fairly specific but most are very broad suggestions. Matching food and wine can be complicated. It is not just about the main constituent of a meal; the sauce, the accompanying vegetables, fruits and herbs all make a difference. I do include quite a few all-purpose wines that can be happily matched with most foods.Instead of simply listing the wines in price order or by country, I think it more useful to divide them up by style; this should make it easier to access the kind of wine you like, and to encourage you to experiment a little. The categories are also colour-coded to aid navigation.

SPARKLING WINES 1-22
Self-explanatory I hope!

CRISP REFRESHING WHITE WINES 23-52
Light, zesty dry white wines with plenty of refreshing acidity. They generally have less alcohol and lighter fruits than those in the Fresh & Fruity category. Good to drink on their own, or with lighter dishes.

FRESH AND FRUITY WHITE WINES 53-94
White wines with plenty of mouth-watering fruits balanced by good acidity. Generally unoaked, with more fruit and flavour than the Crisp Refreshing Whites. Fine to drink on their own or with richer fish and salad dishes.

RICH AND ROUNDED WHITE WINES 95-118

Bigger, more powerful textured white wines, some oak-aged, that fill the mouth with flavour. These wines are best served alongside food.

LIGHT AND ELEGANT RED WINES 119-166

Restrained, lighter wines with more subtle fruits. They are lower in alcohol and have light tannins. These can be drunk on their own or with lighter foods.

ROUNDED AND FRUITY RED WINES 167-212

These red wines have plenty of smooth rounded fruits and moderate tannins; good with many foods.

RICH AND FULL-BODIED RED WINES 213-250

The biggest and most powerful red wines, robust and rich in alcohol and flavour. Some have high levels of tannin too. These wines are best drunk alongside substantial dishes.

FORTIFIED WINES 251-262

Wines such as sherry, port and madeira receive a fortifying boost of brandy to increase their alcohol in the winemaking process. A great many are dry, others are sweet, but don't ignore them - these are amongst the most complex wines of all, and some go really well with food too.

INDEX BY STYLE PRICE COUNTRY

Wine	Price	Country	Page no.
Sparkling Wines			
Philippe Michel Cremant de Jura NV	€ 10.49	France	3
La Rosca Cava Brut NV	€ 14.99	Spain	5
Francesco Drusian Prosecco Colfondo NV	€ 17.95	Italy	7
Beaumont de Crayeres NV Champagne	€ 36.99	France	9
Wiston Estate Blanc de Blancs NV	€ 53.00	UK	11
Larmandier Bernier Latitude Extra Brut NV	€ 59.50	France	13
Nyetimber Classic Cuvée 2010	€ 59.99	UK	15
Champagne Vilmart Grand Cellier Brut, Premier Cru NV Champagne	€ 62.00	France	17
Champagne Deutz Rosé NV Champagne	€ 65.00	France	19
Veuve Cliquot Ponsardin Rosé 2004 Champagne	€ 80.00	France	21
Crisp Refreshing White Wines			
Lombeline Sauvignon Blanc 2014 Vin de Loire	€ 11.00	France	25
Zibibbo 2013, Terre Siciliane	€ 12.29	Italy	27
Custoza 2014 Cantina di Custoza, Veneto	€ 12.95	Italy	29
Sartarelli Verdicchio dei Castelli di Jesi 2014	€ 14.99	Italy	31
Sauvignon Blanc Les Hautes Lieux 2014, Famille Bougrier, Vin de France	€ 15.49	France	33
Muscadet de Sèvre & Maine sur lie, Clos des Montys 2014	€ 15.50	France	35
La Grange Vieilles Vignes 2013 Domaine Luneau-Papin Muscadet de Sèvre & Main Sur Lie	€ 15.95	France	37
Wieninger Wiener Gemischter Satz 2014	€ 17.95	Austria	39
FP Branco 2013, Filipa Pato, IGP Beira Atlantico, Portugal	€ 18.70	Portugal	41
Hunky Dory Sauvignon Blanc 2013, Marlborough	€ 18.99	N Zland	43
Wittmann Riesling 2014, Rheinhessen	€ 22.00	Germany	45
Malat Grüner Veltliner Höhlgraben 2014, Kremstal	€ 23.95	Austria	47
Sancerre Florès 2013 Vincent Pinard	€ 29.50	France	49
Hirsch Kammern Renner Grüner Veltliner 2013, Kamptal	€ 34.95	Austria	51
Fresh & Fruity White wines			
Lidl Cimarosa Marlborough Sauvignon Blanc 2014	€ 8.79	N Zland	55
Domaine de Pellehaut Harmonie de Gascogne 2014	€ 12.99	France	57
Steininger Grüner Veltliner 2014, Kamptal	€ 15.80	Austria	59
Tramin Pinot Grigio 2014, Alto-Adige Sud-Tirol	€ 15.99	Italy	61

Wine	Price	Country	Page no.
Cucu GV Verdejo 2013, Bodega El Barco del Corneta VdT de Castilla y Léon	€ 17.00	Spain	63
Bründlmayer Kamptaler Terrassen Riesling 2013	€ 17.50	Austria	65
Celler Pardas Rupestris 2013, Penedes	€ 17.60	Spain	67
Hugel Cuvée des Amours 2012, Pinot Blanc de Blancs	€ 17.99	France	69
Domaine de Begude Terroir 11300 Chardonnay 2013 Haute Vallée de l'Aude	€ 17.99	France	71
Chardonnay Terres Dorées 2014 Beaujolais Jean-Paul Brun	€ 18.95	France	73
Soalheiro Alvarinho 2014 Vinho Verde	€ 18.99	Portugal	75
Birgit Eichinger Grüner Veltliner Hasel 2014, Kamptal	€ 19.00	Austria	77
Framingham Sauvignon Blanc 2014, Marlborough	€ 19.75	N Zland	79
Blanc d'Ogier 2012, M&S Ogier IGP Collines Rhodaniennes	€ 22.75	France	81
Pazo de Señorans 2013, Rías Baixas	€ 22.99	Spain	83
Dog Point Vineyard Sauvignon Blanc 2014, Marlborough	€ 23.95	N Zland	85
Menade Rueda V3 2013	€ 27.75	Spain	87
Greywacke Wild Sauvignon Blanc 2013, Marlborough	€ 33.00	N Zland	89
Kooyong Chardonnay 2012, Mornington Peninsula	€ 33.95	Australia	91
Mas de Daumas Gassac Blanc 2014, IGP St. Guilhem-le-Desert Cité d'Aniane	€ 45.00	France	93

Rich & Rounded White Wines

Wine	Price	Country	Page no.
El Grano Chardonnay 2013, Poda Corta, Curico Valley (Organic)	€ 15.90	Chile	97
Le Grand Blanc, Comte Phillippe de Bertier 2012	€ 15.95	France	99
Terre d'Eglantier Réserve, Vignerons Ardechois 2013	€ 16.95	France	101
Marc Kreydenweiss Pinot Blanc Kritt 2014, Alsace	€ 17.99	France	103
DMZ Chenin Blanc 2014, DeMorgenzon, Western Cape	€ 18.00	S. Africa	105
Carmen Gran Reserva Chardonnay 2013, Casablanca Valley	€ 18.50	Chile	107
Antão Vaz da Peceguina 2014, Herdade de Malandinha Nova, VR Alentejan	€ 19.95	Portugal	109
Grauburgunder 2013, Wagner Stempel, Rheinhessen	€ 19.95	Germany	111
d'Arenberg Lucky Lizard Chardonnay 2012	€ 22.00	Australia	113
Domaine Larue Puligny-Montrachet 1er cru La Garenne 2013	€ 49.50	France	115
F.X. Pichler Grüner Veltliner Loibner Loibenberg 2012, Wachau	€ 50.00	Austria	117

Wine	Price	Country	Page no.
Light & Elegant Red Wines			
Frunza Pinot Noir 2014, Romania	€ 9.99	Romania	121
Frappato 2013, IGP Terre Siciliane	€ 12.29	Italy	123
Sangoiovese Rubicone Medici Ermete, Emilia-Romagna	€ 12.95	Italy	125
Caves Saint-Désirat Syrah 2013 Vin de pays d'Ardèche	€ 14.49	France	127
Anima Umbra 2012, Arnaldo Caprai, Umbria	€ 14.50	Italy	129
Hacienda Lopez de Haro Rioja Crianza 2011	€ 14.50	Spain	131
La Maldicíon Tinto para beber de Marc Isart 2014 D.O. Madrid	€ 14.50	Spain	133
Carmen Right Wave Leyda Valley Pinot Noir 2014	€ 14.99	Chile	135
Le Salare Montepulciano d'Abruzzo 2013	€ 14.99	Italy	137
Roka Blaufränkisch 2013, Stajerska	€ 15.99	Slovenia	139
Langhe Rosso 2013 Maretti	€ 17.90	Italy	141
J. Regnaudot Bourgogne Pinot Noir 2013	€ 18.25	France	143
Bourgogne Pinot Noir 2013, Patrice Cacheux	€ 19.50	France	145
Castello di Verduna Barbera d'Alba 2013	€ 21.50	Italy	147
Moric Blaufränkisch 2012, Burgenland	€ 22.99	Austria	149
Muhr Van der Niepoort Samt & Seide 2012, Carnuntum	€ 23.00	Austria	151
Ziereisen Tschuppen 2012, Badischer Landwein	€ 24.00	Germany	153
Ka Manciné Rossesse di Dolceacqua Bergana 201	€ 26.00	Italy	155
Fürst Spätburgunder Tradition 2011, Franken	€ 30.00	Germany	157
Greystone Pinot Noir 2012, Waipara	€ 34.00	N Z land	159
Nuits St. Georges 'Les Hauts Pruliers' 2010 Maison Ambroise	€ 46.35	France	161
La Penetencia 2013 Ribera Sacra	€ 50.00	Spain	163
Ata Rangi Pinot Noir 2013, Martinborough	€ 63.99	N Zland	165
Rounded & Fruity Red Wines			
Aranleón Blés Tinto 2014, Valencia	€ 11.00	Spain	169
Perricone Caruso e Minini 2013 Terre Siciliane IGT	€ 12.29	Italy	171
Castro de Valtuille 2013 Bierzo	€ 13.50	Spain	173
Aranleón Encuentro 2014, DOP Valencia	€ 13.99	Spain	175
Oveja Tinta 2014, Bodegas Fontana	€ 13.99	Spain	177
Les Auzines Cuvée Hautes Terres 2011 Corbières	€ 14.49	France	179
Valli Unite 'Ottavio Ruben Rosso' 2013	€ 14.55	Italy	181
Haute Côt(e) de Fruit 2104, Fabien Jouves, Cahors	€ 14.95	France	183
Pegos Claros 2010, Palmela	€ 14.99	Portugal	185
La Malkerida 2012, Utiel-Requena	€ 15.95	Spain	187
7, rue de Pompe 2013, Mas Coutelou, Vin de France	€ 16.50	France	189
Côtes du Rhône Les Deux Cols, Cuvée d'Alizé 2014	€ 16.95	France	191
Tenute Dettori Vino Renosu Rosso NV	€ 17.50	Italy	193

Wine	Price	Country	Page no.
Ch. Sainte-Marie Alios 2012 Côtes de Bordeaux	€ 17.95	France	195
Artuke Pies Negros 2013 Rioja	€ 18.90	Spain	197
Domaine Eian da Ros Abouriou, Côtes du Marmandais 2012	€ 19.50	France	199
Il Molino di Grace 2012 Chianti Classico	€ 19.95	Italy	201
Monte da Peceguina Red 2013, Herdade de Malhadinha Nova	€ 20.95	Portugal	203
Astrolabe Pinot Noir 2010, Marlborough	€ 25.49	N Zland	205
Villa di Capezzana Carmignano 2011	€ 34.99	Italy	207
Santa Rita Casa Real 2011, Maipo Valley	€ 49.95	Chile	209
TolpuddleVineyard Pinot Noir 2013, Tasmania	€ 59.99	Australia	211

Rich & Full-bodied Red Wines

Wine	Price	Country	Page no.
Porta 6 2011 Lisboa	€ 12.99	Portugal	215
Pascual Toso Malbec 2013, Mendoza	€ 13.99	Argentina	217
Rafael Cambra El Bon Homme 2014, Valencia	€ 14.00	Spain	219
Libido 2013 Navarra, David Sampedro Gil	€ 14.50	Spain	221
Dom Rafael 2012, Mouchâo, Alentejo	€ 14.50	Portugal	223
Jean Bousquet Cabernet Sauvignon 2013, Tupungato Valley	€ 15.50	Argentina	225
Le Vin d'Adrien 2014 Domaine de l'Amauve Côtes du Rhône	€ 15.95	France	227
Doña Paula Estate Malbec 2014, Uco Valley	€ 15.99	Argentina	229
Côtes du Rhône 2013, Domaine Saint Gayan	€ 16.95	France	231
Ribeo 2011, Morellino di Scansano, Roccapesta	€ 18.99	Italy	233
Celler Lafou El Sender 2013 Terra Alta	€ 19.95	Spain	235
Gaia S 2010, Koutsi Hillside Vineyard, Peleponnisos	€ 23.49	Greece	237
Quellu' Cinsault 2013 Louis-Antoine Luyt, Curico Valley	€ 23.90	Chile	239
Bodega Colomé Estate 2012, Cafayate	€ 24.99	Argentina	241
Sijnn Red 2010	€ 25.00	S. Africa	243
Ridge East Bench Zinfandel 2013, Dry Creek Valley, Sonoma County, California	€ 29.95	USA	245
Ch. Musar 2007, Bekaa Valley, Lebanon	€ 36.99	Lebannon	247
Casa Emma Chianti Classico Riserva 2010	€ 39.95	Italy	249

Fortified Wines

Wine	Price	Country	Page no.
La Ina Fino Sherry	€ 15.99	Spain	253
Warre's Bottle-aged Late Bottled Port 2003	€ 35.00	Portugal	255
Barbeito 10 Year Old Reserve Sercial Madeira	€ 37.99	Portugal	257
Fonseca Quinta do Panascal Vintage Port 2001	€ 44.95	Portugal	259
Bodegas Tradición Palo Cortado VORS	€ 84.99	Spain	261

SPARKLING WINES

1

Philippe Michel Cremant de Jura NV
France 12% **€10.49**

3

STOCKISTS: Aldi

Philippe Michel Cremant de Jura NV

TASTING NOTE
Rounded red apple fruits, a nice citrus bite and a good finish.

DRINK WITH
Drink with friends at a party.

STYLE
Sparkling

GRAPE VARIETY
Chardonnay

4

BACKSTORY
Tiring of Prosecco? This is one inexpensive alternative; great by itself or as a cocktail base for everything from Buck's Fizz to Kir Royale or something a little more exotic if you fancy a bit of mixology!

2 La Rosca Cava Brut NV
Spain 11.5% **€14.99**

5

STOCKISTS: O'Briens

La Rosca Cava Brut NV

TASTING NOTE
Medium peach and apple fruits with good lively citrus to keep it in check. A prefect Prosecco replacement.

DRINK WITH
For all of those minor celebrations that call for a glass of fizz.

STYLE
Sparkling

GRAPE VARIETY
Macabeo, Parellada, Xarelo

BACKSTORY
As we become a little jaded with Prosecco, it may well be that Cava becomes our next stop for a glass of inexpensive fizz. Produced in large quantities in Catalonia, there are now plenty of well-priced, well-made Cavas to tempt us. This is one such example.

3

Francesco Drusian Prosecco Colfondo NV
Organic
Italy 11% **€17.95**

7

STOCKISTS: Michaels Wines , Deerpark; Quintessential
Wines, Drogheda www.quintessentialwines.ie

Francesco Drusian Prosecco Colfondo NV

TASTING NOTE
Complex crisp pear fruits, with bready, yeasty elements finishing bone dry. Exhilarating wine.

DRINK WITH
Surprise your friends at a party or as a conversation-generating aperitif.

STYLE
Sparkling

GRAPE VARIETY
Glera

BACKSTORY
I dare you to try this wine - it will change your mind about Prosecco. Using organically grown grapes from the family estate, Francesco Drusian makes Prosecco as it was done a hundred years ago, with a second fermentation in the bottle. The result is astonishing and complex; streets ahead of most of its rivals.

4 Beaumont de Crayeres NV Champagne
France 12% €36.99

STOCKISTS: O'Briens

Beaumont de Crayeres
NV Champagne

TASTING NOTE
Ripe, rounded redcurrant and apple fruits and a very decent finish.

DRINK WITH
Fish, shellfish and nibbles. Also works as a good aperitif.

STYLE
Sparkling

GRAPE VARIETY
Chardonnay, Pinot Noir

BACKSTORY
O'Briens has been offering Beaumont de Crayères for many years, and for good reason. The name may not have the recognition factor of the bigger brands, but the wines really stand up - they are well-made and nicely balanced at prices that are very fair. It certainly merits a second appearance here.

5

Wiston Estate Blanc de Blancs NV
England 12% €53

STOCKISTS: Le Caveau, Kilkenny; Bradleys Cork; Corkscrew, Chatham Street; Green Man Wines Terenure; World Wide Wines, Waterford.

Wiston Estate Blanc de Blancs NV

TASTING NOTE
An exquisite combination of racy citrus fruits and toasty brioche, with a lovely long finish.

DRINK WITH
A great partner for oysters or scallops. Alternatively try it with fish and chips - you'll be surprised how good the combination is.

STYLE
Sparkling

GRAPE VARIETY
Chardonnay

BACKSTORY
I featured the delicious rosé from Wiston last year; this time around, their equally tasty blanc de blancs. Limerick-born Irish winemaker Dermot Sugrue is making a name for himself as one of the very best in the U.K. Don't be put off by the price. This is every bit as good as most Champagnes.

6

Larmandier Bernier Latitude Extra Brut NV Champagne
France 12% **€59.50**

STOCKISTS: Terroirs, Donnybrook, terroirs.ie

Larmandier Bernier Latitude Extra Brut NV Champagne

TASTING NOTE
Clean succulent fruits, cut through with a tantalising crisp minerality and a lingering finish.

DRINK WITH
Champagne is one of the great aperitifs, particularly with fish or cheese nibbles, but this would make a great match for fresh Irish oysters.

STYLE
Sparkling

GRAPE VARIETY
Chardonnay, Pinot Noir, Pinot Meunier

BACKSTORY
This wine also featured last year. Pierre and Sophie Larmandier are amongst my favourite Champagne producers, making small quantities of the most precise Champagnes, following biodynamic practices (very unusual in Champagne). Lower levels of residual sugar give their wines an enchanting austere purity.

7

Nyetimber Classic Cuvée 2010
England 12% **€59.99**

STOCKISTS: 64wine, Glasthule; Bradleys, Cork; Cabot & Co. Westport; The Corkscrew, Chatham St.; Donnybrook Fair; Fallon & Byrne, Exchequer St.; Green Man Wines, Terenure; Jus de Vine, Portmarnock; Mitchell & Son, chq & Glasthule; Thomas Woodberry, Galway; The Wine Workshop, D4; Searsons, Monkstown; Thomas, Foxrock.

Nyetimber Classic Cuvée 2010

TASTING NOTE
Exhilarating fresh racy green apples and lemon zest, finishing dry. A magnificent glass of fizz.

DRINK WITH
Before dinner or with a plate of shellfish.

STYLE
Sparkling

GRAPE VARIETY
Chardonnay, Pinot Noir, Pinot Meunier

BACKSTORY
What wine-producing country lies closest to Ireland? Wales actually, with one or two small wineries. But England, and the chalky Sussex Downs has been making a name for it's superb sparkling wines for a number of years. Nyetimber was one of the very first, and remains one of the best.

8

Champagne Vilmart Grand Cellier Brut, Premier Cru NV
France 12% €62

17

STOCKISTS: Quintessential Wines, Drogheda
www.quintessentialwines.ie, Hole in Wall, D7.

Champagne Vilmart Grand Cellier Brut, Premier Cru NV

TASTING NOTE
A beautifully textured elegant Champagne with subtle notes of brioche, rounded fruits, and a refined acidity throughout. Yum!

DRINK WITH
By itself or with nibbles before a nice dinner, or with shellfish.

STYLE
Sparkling

GRAPE VARIETY
Chardonnay, Pinot Noir

BACKSTORY
Vilmart is a grower Champagne, that is, made entirely from grapes grown on the estate. These are becoming very fashionable as drinkers tire a little of the big brands. Vilmart is also one of the very best. The family have been making Champagne in the Montagne de Reims region since 1890.

9 Champagne Deutz Rosé NV
France 12% €65

19

STOCKISTS: La Touche, Greystones; The Corkscrew, Chatham St.; Village Off-Licence, Castleknock; The Wine Centre, Kilkenny; 64 Wine, Glasthule; Wine On Line.

Champagne Deutz Rosé NV

TASTING NOTE
Discreet refined raspberry and strawberry fruits;
refreshing and dry.

DRINK WITH
To sip before dinner, or with fish and white meats.

STYLE
Sparkling

GRAPE VARIETY
Pinot Noir, Pinot Meunier, Chardonnay

BACKSTORY
Deutz is owned by the famous Champagne house of
Louis Roederer. However, the two companies are run
completely independently. Roederer is probably better-
known, but Deutz has its own distinctive delicious style.

10

**Veuve Cliquot
Ponsardin Rosé 2004
Champagne**
France 12% €80

STOCKISTS: Celtic Whiskey Store, Redmond's, O'Briens
and Jus de Vine, Portmarnock.

Veuve Cliquot Ponsardin Rosé 2004 Champagne

TASTING NOTE
Quite delicious mature refined raspberry fruits, balanced perfectly by the acidity. Elegant and sophisticated; excellent Champagne.

DRINK WITH
On its own for that special celebration or with veal and chicken dishes.

STYLE
Sparkling

GRAPE VARIETY
Pinot Noir

BACKSTORY
There is something special about rosé Champagne; it combines the luxury and style associated with Champagne with an added seductive fruitiness. It is also frequently a great wine to drink with food. I was lucky enough to taste this wine twice over the last year; on both occasions I was mightily impressed.

CRISP
REFRESHING
WHITE WINES

11

Lombeline Sauvignon Blanc 2014 Vin de Loire
France 12% €11

STOCKISTS: La Touche, Greystones; Jus de Vine, Portmarnock; McCabes, Blackrock & Foxrock; Rua, Castelbar; Liston's, Camden St.

Lombeline Sauvignon Blanc 2014 Vin de Loire

TASTING NOTE
Herby, grassy aromas and fresh clean green fruits with a nice zesty kick.

DRINK WITH
Before dinner, with fishy starters or mild goat's cheese salad.

STYLE
Crisp Refreshing White Wines

GRAPE VARIETY
Sauvignon Blanc

BACKSTORY
Lombeline is selected by Charles Derain, former sommelier at Restaurant Patrick Guilbaud. As well as bringing in an excellent range of fine Burgundy and a few other goodies, he sources this Loire Sauvignon. We all need a house white, something reliable that we can crack open and enjoy before dinner or with a starter. The Lombeline fits into this category perfectly; inexpensive, well-made and satisfying every time.

12

Zibibbo 2013, Terre Siciliane
Italy 12% **€12.29**

STOCKISTS: Marks & Spencer

Zibibbo 2013, Terre Siciliane

TASTING NOTE
Delicious floral, scented, crisp dry white wine with plump green fruits and a zesty finish.

DRINK WITH
On its own before dinner or for sipping with friends.

STYLE
Crisp Refreshing White Wines

GRAPE VARIETY
Zibibbo

BACKSTORY
Zibibbo is believed to be a clone of Muscat of Alexandria, one of the oldest of all grape varieties. The lifted fresh grapey aromas will certainly remind you of Muscat, but, unlike most Muscat, this also has plenty of mouth-watering citrus acidity. Perfect everyday drinking at a great price.

13 Custoza 2014 Cantina di Custoza, Veneto
Italy 12% **€12.95**

STOCKISTS: Bean & Berry, Wexford; Blackrock Cellar; The Corkscrew, Chatham St.; Listons, Camden St.; Hole in the Wall; D7; Morton's, Ranelagh; SuperValu, Sutton; Nectar Wines, Sandyford; Michael's, Deerpark; The Wicklow Wine Co.

Custoza 2014 Cantina di Custoza, Veneto

TASTING NOTE
A well-made light crisp fresh dry white from Italy. Better than most Pinot Grigio in this price range; a great everyday option.

DRINK WITH
By itself or with light fish dishes and shellfish.

STYLE
Crisp Refreshing White Wines

GRAPE VARIETY
Tocai Friulano, Garganega, Riesling Italico, Chardonnay, Trebbiano Toscano

BACKSTORY
Custoza (once Bianco di Custoza) is one of the lesser-known names from the Veneto in north-east Italy. I have always been very fond of its wines. They fall into a category that the Italians do very well; light and zesty whites to drink with fish. They prefer these to wines with too much aroma or flavour – sort of like a vinous squeeze of lemon to go with plainly cooked fish served hot or cold with a few herbs and maybe some olive oil.

14

Sartarelli Verdicchio dei Castelli di Jesi 2014
Italy 13% **€14.99/£9.95**

STOCKISTS: Jnwine.com

Sartarelli Verdicchio dei Castelli di Jesi 2014

TASTING NOTE
A wonderful combination of light and fresh with rich fruit. Clean citrus with peaches and pears finishing dry. Exceptional value for money.

DRINK WITH
Perfect with plain seafood dishes.

STYLE
Crisp refreshing white wines

GRAPE VARIETY
Verdicchio

BACKSTORY
Verdicchio often can be fairly neutral; easy to drink but nothing to get excited about. However, in the right hands, it can produce some beautifully rich yet refreshing dry whites. The Sartarelli family are certainly the right hands. In this book for a second year, this is one of those wines that instantly will put a smile on your face. It doesn't cost the earth either.

15

Sauvignon Blanc Les Hautes Lieux 2014, Famille Bougrier, Vin de France
France 12% **€15.49**

STOCKISTS: O'Briens

Sauvignon Blanc Les Hautes Lieux 2014, Famille Bougrier, Vin de France

TASTING NOTE
Floral, herby aromas, followed on by light lipsmacking clean green fruits, with a crisp dry finish

DRINK WITH
By itself or with a salad of mild goat's cheese.

STYLE
Crisp refreshing white wines

GRAPE VARIETY
Sauvignon Blanc

BACKSTORY
We are all familiar with Marlborough Sauvignon from New Zealand. But the Loire Valley has been growing this grape variety for centuries, and does it very well. The wines tend to be a little less aromatic, but have the same refreshing vibrant green fruits, often at very keen prices. This wine also featured in last year's book. O'Briens promotes this wine at €9.99 periodically when it becomes an amazing bargain.

16

**Muscadet de Sèvre & Maine
sur lie, Clos des Montys 2014**
France 12% €15.50

STOCKISTS: Jus de Vine, Portmarnock; Redmonds,
Ranelagh; One Pery Sq. Limerick; 64wine, Glasthule.

Muscadet de Sèvre & Maine sur lie, Clos des Montys 2014

TASTING NOTE
Clean, subtle, almost snow-like with crisp green apple fruits, a lovely long mineral finish and a light spritz.

DRINK WITH
Perfection with oysters and other shellfish.

STYLE
Crisp Refreshing White Wines

GRAPE VARIETY
Melon de Bourgogne

BACKSTORY
I was introduced to Jeremie Huchet at a wine fair in Germany earlier this year, and was hugely impressed by him and his wines. He makes a string of Muscadets, both from his own estates and for other vineyard owners. All of them were excellent, none more so than this wine.

17

**Muscadet Sèvre & Main Sur Lie
La Grange Vieilles Vignes
2013 Domaine Luneau-Papin**
France 12% **€15.95**

STOCKISTS: Whelehan's Wines, Loughlinstown

Muscadet Sèvre & Main Sur Lie La Grange Vieilles Vignes 2013 Domaine Luneau-Papin

TASTING NOTE
Delectable, pristine tangy pear fruits wrapped around a stony mineral core.

DRINK WITH
Perfection with oysters and other shellfish.

STYLE
Crisp Refreshing White Wines

GRAPE VARIETY
Melon de Bourgogne

BACKSTORY
Is Muscadet making a comeback? I certainly hope so. I love those exhilarating racy, bracing fresh flavours that go so well with seafood. It seems our tastes are switching to lighter, more refreshing wines and Muscadet is one of the very best.

18

Wieninger Wiener Gemischter Satz 2014
Austria 12.5% **€17.95**

STOCKISTS: On the Grapevine Dalkey; World Wide Wines, Waterford; Thomas Woodberry's, Galway; McFaddens, Letterkenny; The Corkscrew @ Kenny's Lucan; The Corkscrew, Chatham Street.

Wieninger Wiener Gemischter Satz 2014

TASTING NOTE
Delectable racy wine with appetising green fruits and a subtle touch of ginger, finishing dry. Different and well worth seeking out.

DRINK WITH
A very enjoyable aperitif or with lighter seafood dishes.

STYLE
Crisp Refreshing White Wines

GRAPE VARIETY
More than 20 different grape varieties.

BACKSTORY
Fritz Wieninger and his family grow vines up in the hills surrounding Vienna. They also run a Heurige, a Viennese tradition of winery/pub/wine bar that offers wine by the glass or bottle along with some food. Fritz has taken the winemaking side into a different league and is today the best producer in Vienna and one of the greatest in Austria. 'Gemischter Satz' is made from a field blend of many different grape varieties all grown side by side in the same vineyards. This delicious fresh spring-like wine is exactly the kind of thing you would love to come across in a Heurige.

19

FP Branco 2013, Filipa Pato, IGP Beira Atlantico
Portugal 13% €18.70

STOCKISTS: Blackrock Cellar; Black Pig, Donnybrook; Baggot Street wines; 64wine, Glasthule; Ennis Butchers, South Circular Road; Green Man Wines, Terenure.

FP Branco 2013, Filipa Pato, IGP Beira Atlantico

TASTING NOTE
Delectable and pure fresh white peach and citrus zest
with an appealing subtle creaminess.

DRINK WITH
Mussels in white wine with herbs.

STYLE
Crisp Refreshing White Wines

GRAPE VARIETY
Arinto, Bical

BACKSTORY
Filipa Pato is the daughter of Luis Pato, one of Portugal's
foremost wine producers. Instead of joining the family
business, however, she travelled the world for a few years
to gain experience before setting up her own company.
She has inherited her father's love of traditional grapes.
Using these, she fashions a series of quirky, free-flowing
fresh wines that are a joy to drink. I recommended the red
version of this wine last year, and would certainly suggest
you keep an eye out for it as well.

20

Hunky Dory Sauvignon Blanc 2013, Marlborough
New Zealand 13% €18.99
Organic

STOCKISTS: Ardkeen, Waterford; Carpenters, Castleknock; Blackrock Cellar; LaTouche, Greystones; No. 21 Midleton, Cork; O'Driscolls, Cahirciveen; The Wine Centre, Kilkenny.

Hunky Dory Sauvignon Blanc 2013, Marlborough

TASTING NOTE
Lifted elderflowers and herbs with luscious exotic fruits finishing dry.

DRINK WITH
Very good with herby Asian fish dishes or fresh goat's cheese salads.

STYLE
Crisp Refreshing White Wines

GRAPE VARIETY
Sauvignon Blanc

BACKSTORY
Mike and Claire Allen met while studying winemaking, and, having worked for a few other wineries and saved some money, set up Huia almost 20 years ago. The Huia vineyards are now farmed biodynamically. The Huia Sauvignon is one of Marlborough's best, while the Hunky Dory, made from their neighbour's vineyards, offers cracking value.

21

Wittmann Riesling 2014, Rheinhessen
Germany 12% **€22**
Organic

STOCKISTS: Cabot and Co, Westport (www.cabotandco.com); On the Grapevine, Dalkey (www.onthegrapevine.ie); No.1 Pery Square, Limerick; Mortons of Galway.

Wittmann Riesling 2014, Rheinhessen

TASTING NOTE
Lifted floral aromas, with flowing white peach fruits on the palate cut though by delicate but persistent minerals and lime.

DRINK WITH
Prawns or other shellfish, or lighter Chinese foods.

STYLE
Crisp Refreshing White Wines

GRAPE VARIETY
Riesling

BACKSTORY
Although the Wittmann estate has been in operation since the 1660s, it is only since Phillip Wittmann took over some 20 years ago that its reputation has soared. He has long been an advocate of organics, and has been biodynamic since 2004. He is self-effacing, arguing his wonderful terroir is responsible for the wines. The vineyards are completely removed from the steep rocky slopes along the Rhine and Mosel. They are gently undulating and rich in clay. Wittmann explains that it is the loess topsoil that gives the vines perfect drainage. The wines are elegant and mineral, but with no shortage of rich fruit. The best wines are exquisite but, sadly, expensive too. However, this Riesling is one of my favourties.

22 Malat Grüner Veltliner Höhlgraben 2014, Kremstal
Austria 12.5% **€23.95**

STOCKISTS: Searsons, Monkstown

Malat Grüner Veltliner Höhlgraben 2014, Kremstal

TASTING NOTE
Classic Grüner Veltliner spice and plump melon fruits,
finishing dry. Delectable clean refreshing wine.

DRINK WITH
Drink by itself, with seafood, or herby salads.

STYLE
Crisp Refreshing White Wines

GRAPE VARIETY
Grüner Veltliner

BACKSTORY
Michael Malat, like his father before him, makes a
bewildering number of wines, most very good, and a
few excellent, from a huge number of grape varieties.
The sparkling wines and reds are very fine, but I always
make a beeline for his outstanding Rieslings and Grüner
Veltliners. Great to see they are now available in Ireland.
If you fancy really breaking out, try the Alte Reben (or old
vine) Höhlgraben for €32.

23 **Sancerre Florès 2013**
Vincent Pinard
France 13% **€29.50**

49

STOCKISTS: Terroirs, Donnybrook, terroirs.ie; jnwine.com

Sancerre Florès 2013
Vincent Pinard

TASTING NOTE
A stunning Sancerre with lifted floral aromas, and a superb razor-sharp, clean refined mineral palate, finishing bone dry. Sauvignon at its very best.

DRINK WITH
Herby fish dishes. I had mine with hake in a creamy dill sauce and peas.

STYLE
Crisp Refreshing Whites

GRAPE VARIETY
Sauvignon Blanc

BACKSTORY
For some time now, I have been bored with the sea of unexciting Sancerres in just about every wine shop. Then every now and again, you come across one that reminds you just how good they can be. Vincent Pinard crafts a series of excellent white wines using different techniques, as well as three red wines from Pinot Noir. All come under the Sancerre name. I have only once tasted the Pinot, but his white wines are amongst the very best in Sancerre.

24

Hirsch Kammern Renner Grüner Veltliner 2013, Kamptal
Austria 12.5% **€34.95**

STOCKISTS: The Corkscrew @ Kenny's Lucan;
The Corkscrew Chatham St., D 2.

Hirsch Kammern Renner Grüner Veltliner 2013, Kamptal

TASTING NOTE
Succulent flowing textured peach and orange fruits with excellent clean length.

DRINK WITH
Perfect as an aperitif or with Asian seafood dishes.

STYLE
Crisp Refreshing White Wines

GRAPE VARIETY
Grüner Veltliner

BACKSTORY
I have been visiting the Hirsch stand at Vievinum, the great biennial Austrian wine fair, for many years now. I have a soft spot for the Kamptal anyway – its more elegant refreshing style is right up my street, and the region boasts some of Austria's greatest producers – Scloss Gobelsburg, Bründlmayer, Loimer, Jurtschitsch and others besides. I have always put Johannes Hirsch right up there with the very best, and it is great to see his wines return to Ireland after a few years absence.

FRESH AND FRUITY
WHITE WINES

25

**Cimarosa Marlborough
Sauvignon Blanc 2014**
New Zeland12.5% **€8.79**

55

STOCKISTS: Lidl

Cimarosa Marlborough Sauvignon Blanc 2014

TASTING NOTE
Fresh and light with good lifted herby aromas, light fresh green fruits and classic Marlborough citrus acidity.

DRINK WITH
Ideal for sipping with friends or with salads and fish.

STYLE
Fresh & Fruity White Wines

GRAPE VARIETY
Sauvignon Blanc

BACKSTORY
Visiting the massive (1,000 hectare) Yealands estate in Marlborough a few months ago, I spied a bottle of this wine in the tasting room. Peter Yealands smiled and said, yes we do supply a Sauvignon to Lidl. It is not the same cuvée as the Peter Yealands, which sells for around €15, but those on a limited budget who enjoy Marlborough Sauvignon should certainly stock up on this wine.

26 Domaine de Pellehaut
Harmonie de Gascogne 2014
France 11% **€12.99**

STOCKISTS: Mitchell & Son, IFSC, Sandycove and Avoca, Kilmacanogue; Deveney's; Thyme Out, Dalkey; Myles Doyle, Gorey..

Domaine de Pellehaut Harmonie de Gascogne 2014

TASTING NOTE
Aromatic and lively with rich herby peach fruits and a touch of honey.

DRINK WITH
Perfect for sipping before dinner with friends or at a party.

STYLE
Fresh & Fruity White Wines

GRAPE VARIETY
Ugni Blanc, Sauvignon Blanc, Chardonnay, Gros & Petit Manseng, Folle Blanche, Colombard.

BACKSTORY
It sounds like a kitchen sink wine, with a blend of no less than seven different grape varieties, but somehow it works, and works really well too. Domaine de Pellehaut, down in deepest south-west France, originally produced Armagnac, one of the great brandies. Like many such estates, they now produce a range of red, white and rosé wines.

27 Steininger Grüner Veltliner 2014, Kamptal
Austria 12.5% **€15.80**

STOCKISTS: Wines Direct, Mullingar winesdirect.ie

Steininger Grüner Veltliner 2014, Kamptal

TASTING NOTE
A perfect example of the lighter refreshing style of Grüner, with green apple fruits and a crisp dry finish.

DRINK WITH
Grüner Veltliner is one of the great food wines, happy to partner a wide variety of fish, chicken, veal and pork dishes, including a great many Asian dishes.

STYLE
Fresh & Fruity White Wines

GRAPE VARIETY
Grüner Veltliner

BACKSTORY
Steininger is better known in Austria as a sparkling wine producer, but I have always found the still wines to be very good and very fairly priced too. Grüner Veltliner is becoming very fashionable in wine bars and restaurants around Ireland. If you haven't tried it yet, now is the time to do so.

28 Tramin Pinot Grigio 2014, Alto-Adige Sud-Tirol
Italy 13% **€15.99**

STOCKISTS: Jus de Vine, Portmarnock; Wines on the Green; McCabes, Blackrock; Fresh, Grand Canal St.; Probus, Fenian St.; 64 Wine; Baggot Street Wines; Blackrock Cellar; Clontarf Wines; Gibneys, Malahide; Martins, Fairview; Nolans, Clontarf; The Vintry, Dublin 6.

Tramin Pinot Grigio 2014, Alto-Adige Sud-Tirol

TASTING NOTE
A very appetising fresh wine with lively pear fruits, a touch of ginger spice, nicely textured throughout and good length.

DRINK WITH
Serve with antipasti, or creamy seafood pasta dishes.

STYLE
Fresh & Fruity White Wines

GRAPE VARIETY
Pinot Grigio

BACKSTORY
The vast majority of Pinot Grigio wine tastes light, fruity and inoffensive – at best. There is nothing wrong with that, but if you pay a few euros more, you will be amazed at the leap in quality. This is one such example. Cantina Tramin is a co-operative of 300 growers based in Termeno in the foothills of the Alps. They made their name producing a series of very high-quality aromatic white wines.

29 **Cucu GV Verdejo 2013,
Bodega El Barco del
Corneta VdT de Castilla
y Léon**
Spain 13% **€17** Organic

STOCKISTS: Black Pig, Donnybrook; 64Wines,
Glasthule; Green Man Wines, Terenure; Baggot Street
Wines; Clontarf Wines; Drinkstore, Manor Street; Ennis
Butchers, South Circular Rd.

Cucu GV Verdejo 2013, Bodega El Barco del Corneta VdT de Castilla y Léon

TASTING NOTE
A thrilling mix of grapefruit, pineapples and herbs with a stiff backbone of acidity. Streets ahead of most Rueda.

DRINK WITH
All kinds of shellfish and seafood.

STYLE
Fresh & Fruity White Wines

GRAPE VARIETY
Verdejo

BACKSTORY
Beatriz Herranz set up this winery on her family's estate, having first worked in other areas of Spain. The grapes are organically grown. This is only her second vintage, but she is already winning over the critics. Although all of the vineyards are in Rueda, she prefers to use the wider D.O. of Castilla y Léon.

30

Bründlmayer Kamptaler Terrassen Riesling 2013
Austria 13% €17.50

STOCKISTS: Greenacres, Wexford.

Bründlmayer Kamptaler Terrassen Riesling 2013

TASTING NOTE
A sophisticated racy wine with lively refreshing citrus and green fruits, and a long dry mineral finish.

DRINK WITH
Lighter chicken dishes or shellfish.

STYLE
Fresh & Fruity White Wines

GRAPE VARIETY
Riesling

BACKSTORY
Willi Bründlmayer is one of Austria's greatest winemakers. He produces a string of wines, some very good, others brilliant. A visit to the Bründlmayer stand at a wine fair takes time, but is always worth it. The range is breathtaking; red wines, an excellent sparkling wine, as well as Chardonnay, Pinot Blanc and Pinot Gris. But the highlights are always to be found amongst the Rieslings and Grüner Veltliners, a series of thrilling complex wines, each echoing the vineyards from which they spring.

31

**Celler Pardas Rupestris
2013, Penedes**
Spain 13% €17.50

STOCKISTS: 64Wine, Glasthule; Clontarf Wines; Green
Man Wines, Terenure; Baggot Street Wines; Michael's
Food & Wine,Deerpark; La Touche Wines, Greystones.

Celler Pardas Rupestris 2013, Penedes

TASTING NOTE
A fascinating wine with baked gooseberries, peaches and honeycomb, finishing bone dry.

DRINK WITH
A Catalan fish stew.

STYLE
Fresh & Fruity White Wines

GRAPE VARIETY
Xarello, Red Xarello, Malvasia di Sitges

BACKSTORY
This small estate, set up by winemaker Ramon Perera and viticulturist Jordi Arnan, specialises in Xarello (or Xare-lo, or Xarel.lo as they call it). This Catalan grape is normally used to make Cava, the Spanish sparkling wine. The exquisite Celler Pardas wines are evidence that it can also produce seriously good still wines too.

32 Hugel Cuvée des Amours 2012, Pinot Blanc de Blancs
France 12% **€17.99**

STOCKISTS: The Vintry, Rathmines, Redmond's, Ranelagh; Jus de Vine, Portmarnock; Clontarf Wines; Shiels, Malahide

Hugel Cuvée des Amours 2012, Pinot Blanc de Blancs

TASTING NOTE
Light in body with gentle apple and quince fruits with a clean refreshing acidity.

DRINK WITH
Perfect sipping wine or with salads and lighter fish dishes.

STYLE
Fresh & Fruity White Wines

GRAPE VARIETY
Pinot Blanc, Pinot Auxerrois

BACKSTORY
Pinot Blanc generally gets a pretty bad press, rated lower than Pinot Gris/Grigio, which isn't saying much. 'Useful rather than exciting', according to Jancis Robinson. I think this is a little unfair. I enjoy the soft easy fruitiness you get from Pinot Blanc and its cousin Auxerrois and usually prefer them to Pinot Gris/Grigio. They also make fantastic party wines.

33

**Domaine de Begude
Terroir 11300 Chardonnay
2013 Haute Vallée de l'Aude**
France 13% **€17.99** Organic

STOCKISTS: O'Briens

Domaine de Begude Terroir 11300 Chardonnay 2013 Haute Vallée de l'Aude

TASTING NOTE
Wonderful pure peach and apple fruits, hints of toasted nuts and a long mineral finish.

DRINK WITH
This would be ideal with salmon, black sole or roast chicken. .

STYLE
Fresh & Fruity White Wines

GRAPE VARIETY
Chardonnay

BACKSTORY
I am a huge fan of Englishman James Kinglake's basic white wine - Le Bel Ange, which featured in last year's edition. However, Domaine de Begude also produces several more expensive wines, including this delicious Chardonnay, which has been partially aged in new oak barrels. It is certainly not over-oaked though; this is beautifully balanced wine at a great price. 11300 refers to the local postcode.

34

Chardonnay Terres Dorées
2014 Beaujolais
Jean-Paul Brun
France 12% **€18.95** Organic

STOCKISTS: Wines Direct

Chardonnay Terres Dorées 2014 Beaujolais Jean-Paul Brun

TASTING NOTE
A wonderfully subtle wine with appetising fresh apple and citrus and a touch of honey in the background.

DRINK WITH
Perfect served on its own, but a great match for lighter fish dishes.

STYLE
Fresh & Fruity White Wines

GRAPE VARIETY
Chardonnay

BACKSTORY
The 2012 was in last year, and the 2014 is a worthy successor. This is one of my desert island wines. With perfectly formed pure fruits and no oak whatsoever, it is essence of Chardonnay. Even if you do not generally like this variety, I would urge you to try this wine; it is that good.

35 Soalheiro Alvarinho 2014 Vinho Verde
Portugal 12.5% **€18.99/£12.99**

STOCKISTS: jnwine.com

Soalheiro Alvarinho 2014 Vinho Verde

TASTING NOTE
A good follow-on from the excellent 2013 vintage, the 2014 is a vivid lively wine with succulent pear fruits and a zesty dry finish.

DRINK WITH
Fish & shellfish

STYLE
Fresh & Fruity White Wines

GRAPE VARIETY
Alvarinho

BACKSTORY
Alvarinho in northern Portugal is Albariño over the border in Galicia in Spain. Both make delicious refreshing wines dripping with mouth-watering pear fruits. At one stage Vinho Verde was something you only drank on holiday in Portugal; these days it can be a seriously good dry white wine. This wine appears for a second time; it is one of my favourite white wines.

36 Birgit Eichinger Grüner Veltliner Hasel 2014
Austria 12% **€19**

STOCKISTS: Redmonds, Ranelagh; Mitchell & Son, IFSC, Glasthule and Avoca, Kilmacanogue.

Birgit Eichinger Grüner Veltliner Hasel 2014

TASTING NOTE
From one of my favourite producers, a delectable flowing wine with subtle spicy peach fruits, finishing dry.

DRINK WITH
This would go nicely with a wide variety of foods; try it with Chinese and Japanese fish, seafood and chicken recipies.

STYLE
Fresh & Fruity White Wines

GRAPE VARIETY
Grüner Veltliner

BACKSTORY
Birgit Eichinger is one of a handful of female Austrian winemakers. She runs the entire enterprise herself - office, cellar and winemaking. She also set up a marketing co-operative called 11 Wein Frauen or 11 women winemakers, which has been very successful. In a very short period she has established herself as one of Austria's best producers. I love the way her wines always have the perfect weight of plump seductive fruit that makes you want another sip, and then another...

37

Framingham Sauvignon Blanc 2014, Marlborough
New Zealand 13% **€19.75**

STOCKISTS: Le Caveau, Kilkenny; Fallon and Byrne, Exchequer St.; Green Man Wines, Terenure; World Wide Wines, Waterford.

Framingham Sauvignon Blanc 2014, Marlborough

TASTING NOTE
Complex wine with subtle flavours of peach, grilled nuts and a very fine mineral finish.

DRINK WITH
Chicken salad or a herby creamy goat's cheese salad.

STYLE
Fresh & Fruity White Wines

GRAPE VARIETY
Sauvignon Blanc

BACKSTORY
Framingham is not the best known producer in Marlborough, but it releases some excellent wines. Most wine lovers would have a high regard for its Rieslings, but I was very taken with the Sauvignon, a wine that has much more interest than the standard Marlborough version. The winemaking team are all very fond of punk rock too. On my visit there, we spent as much time discussing the Ramones as Marlborough wines.

38 Blanc d'Ogier 2012, M&S Ogier IGP Collines Rhodaniennes
France 12.5% **€22.75**

STOCKISTS: Donnybrook Fair; 64wine, Glasthule; The Drink Store, D7

Blanc d'Ogier 2012, M&S
Ogier IGP Collines Rhodaniennes

TASTING NOTE
A delightful combination of sophisticated exotic peach fruits and spring-fresh light acidity.

DRINK WITH
The perfect posh aperitif or with creamy chicken dishes.

STYLE
Fresh & Fruity White Wines

GRAPE VARIETY
Viognier, Marsanne, Roussanne

BACKSTORY
Stéphane Ogier is one of the brightest young winemakers in the Rhône Valley, responsible for a series of incredible wines from the very posh appellation of Côte Rôtie. Fortunately for us he also makes a few less expensive wines that while not cheap, offer fantastic value. The red version of this, made from Syrah, is also excellent. Sadly the importer was between vintages as we went to press.

39

Pazo de Señorans
2013, Rías Baixas
Spain 12.5% **€22.99**

STOCKISTS: O'Briens

Pazo de Señorans
2013, Rías Baixas

TASTING NOTE
Plump succulent pear fruits, cut through by firm citrussy minerals. Excellent wine.

DRINK WITH
Great with all things fishy, but scallops would be my favourite choice.

STYLE
Fresh & Fruity White Wines

GRAPE VARIETY
Albariño

BACKSTORY
The vineyards of Rías Baixas, strung along the north-western coast of Spain produce some delicious fruit-filled zingy whites that go perfectly with the local seafood. Scallops and Albariño are a match made in heaven. Look out for other Galician whites, such as Valdeorras, Monterrei and Ribeiro. But back to Pazo de Señorans; this is one of the very best wines of Galicia.

40

**Dog Point Vineyard
Sauvignon Blanc 2014,
Marlborough**
New Zealand 13% **€23.95**

STOCKISTS: Jnwine.com; Corkscrew; Whelehan'ss
Wines, Loughlinstown; The Counter, Letterkenny;
Hardagons, Sligo; Power & Smullen, Lucan, Dicey
Reilly's, Ballyshannon.

Dog Point Vineyard Sauvignon Blanc 2014, Marlborough

TASTING NOTE
Precise refined tropical fruits with perfectly measured mouth-watering citrus acidity.

DRINK WITH
Seafood, chicken dishes or fresh goat's cheese.

STYLE
Fresh & Fruity White Wines

GRAPE VARIETY
Sauvignon Blanc

BACKSTORY
Dog Point is owned by Ivan and Margaret Sutherland and James and Wendy Healy, who were heavily involved in setting up New Zealand's best-known producer, Cloudy Bay. Now they make their own excellent Sauvignon Blanc, as well as allowing Kevin Judd (former Cloudy Bay winemaker) produce his Greywacke wines (also in this book) in the winery.

41 Menade Rueda V3 2012
Spain 13% **€27.75** Organic

STOCKISTS: Le Caveau, Kilkenny; Ballymaloe School Garden Shop; Corkscrew, Chatham Street; 64 wines, Glasthule.

Menade Rueda V3 2012

TASTING NOTE
An explosion of minerals, crisp green fruits with a strong herby element. Long and very dry. Great wine.

DRINK WITH
Seafood paella.

STYLE
Fresh and fruity

GRAPE VARIETY
Verdejo

BACKSTORY
I first came across Richard Sanz some 20 years ago, when he was making large quantities of very modern Rueda in the family business. He disappeared from view for a while but then reappeared with a new enterprise, co-owned with his brother and sister. Here they make some beautiful pure wines, including the stunning V3. Expensive but worth it.

42

Greywacke Wild Sauvignon Blanc 2013, Marlborough
New Zealand 13% **€33**

STOCKISTS: Blackrock Cellar; Clontarf Wines; The Corkscrew, Chatham St.; Donnybrook Fair; Fine Wines, nationwide; Green Man Wines, Terenure; Redmond's, Ranelagh; Jus de Vine, Portmarnock; Londis, Malahide; Mannings Emporium, Ballylickey; Martin's, Fairview; Mitchell & Son, chq, Sandycove & Avoca, Kilmacanogue; Wineonline.ie; World Wide Wines, Waterford.

Greywacke Wild Sauvignon Blanc 2013, Marlborough

TASTING NOTE
A wonderful young wine with lifted complex aromas of lime zest, flowers and cut grass. Beautifully balanced and precise with luscious ripe peaches balanced perfectly by a zesty acidity and a subtle toastiness.

DRINK WITH
Best with fish dishes or herby salads, but great on its own too.

STYLE
Fresh & Fruity White Wines

GRAPE VARIETY
Sauvignon Blanc

BACKSTORY
This wine also featured in last year's edition, but this is hardly surprising as it is made by one of New Zealand's greatest producers. In fact, Kevin Judd was born and reared in Australia, but now considers himself a Kiwi. Having made his name at Cloudy Bay, he moved on to found Greywacke, whose wines are made in the winery at Dog Point, a wine that also features in this book.

91

STOCKISTS: Whelehan's Wines, Loughlinstown

Kooyong Chardonnay 2012, Mornington Peninsula

TASTING NOTE
Superbly crafted pristine wine with wonderful pure apple fruits, a touch of toasty oak, and a long lemony finish.

DRINK WITH
Seared scallops with something herby or pea purée.

STYLE
Fresh & Fruity White Wines

GRAPE VARIETY
Chardonnay

BACKSTORY
The Mornington Peninsula, an hour's drive along the coast from Melbourne, produces some of the most elegant and refined Pinot Noir and Chardonnay in Australia. This wine is made by Sandro Mosele, one of the most respected winemakers in the region, at the spectacular modern Mount Phillip Estate.

44

Mas de Daumas Gassac Blanc 2014, IGP St. Guilhem -le-Desert Cité d'Aniane
France 13.5% **€45**

93

STOCKISTS: Red Nose Wines, Clonmel; Curious Wines, Cork; On the Grapevine, Dalkey.

Mas de Daumas Gassac Blanc 2014, IGP St. Guilhem -le-Desert Cité d'Aniane

TASTING NOTE
A wonderfully elegant wine with enticing floral aromas and soft juicy white peach fruits.

DRINK WITH
Chicken salad or maybe some prawns.

STYLE
Fresh & Fruity White Wines

GRAPE VARIETY
Chardonnay, Viognier, Gros Manseng, Bhenin Blanc and other local grape varieties.

BACKSTORY
Last year I featured the wonderful and celebrated red wine from this estate. The white wine may not enjoy quite the same fame, but I have always enjoyed its fresh but plump mellow fruits and orange peel acidity. An eclectic make-up of varieties that varies from year to year.

RICH AND ROUNDED WHITE WINES

45 **El Grano Chardonnay
2013, Poda Corta,
Curico Valley**
Chile 13% **€15.90** Organic

STOCKISTS: Le Caveau, Kilkenny; Baggot Street Wines;
Blackrock Cellar; 64 wine, Glasthule; Green Man Wines,
Terenure.

El Grano Chardonnay 2013, Poda Corta, Curico Valley

TASTING NOTE
Nicely textured wine with subtle toast and very tasty ripe tropical fruits.

DRINK WITH
With spicy chicken or prawns.

STYLE
Rich & Rounded White Wines

GRAPE VARIETY
Chardonnay

BACKSTORY
In 1991, Denis Duveau sold his property in the Loire Valley and instead began advising producers in France and elsewhere. In 2002, he set up a winery in the Curico Valley in Chile, determined to make terroir-driven organic wine. In 2006, he was joined by his son Grégoire who looks after the organic vineyards in the dry valley. The Chardonnay stands out as something special in a sea of well-made but very similar wines.

46

Le Grand Blanc, Comte Phillippe de Bertier 2012
France 13% **€15.95**

STOCKISTS: Molloy's Liquor Stores

Le Grand Blanc, Comte Phillippe de Bertier 2012

TASTING NOTE
A maturing wine that is showing some real style.
Peaches in custard with a smooth mellow texture.

DRINK WITH
I would try this out with creamy chicken dishes.

STYLE
Rich & Rounded White Wines

100

GRAPE VARIETY
Chardonnay, Roussanne, Viognier

BACKSTORY
It shouldn't work but it does. An improbable blend of
Chardonnay, Roussanne and Viognier, aged in new oak
barrels, this has come together very nicely into a different
but very seductive wine.

47
Viognier Terre d'Eglantier Réserve Vignerons Ardechois 2013
France 14% **€16.95**

STOCKISTS: Red Island Wine, Skerries; Hole in the Wall, D7; Deveneys, Rathmines; The Wicklow Wine Co.

Viognier Terre d'Eglantier Réserve, Vignerons Ardechois 2013

TASTING NOTE
Rich textured peach and apricot fruits overlaid with grilled nuts and toast.

DRINK WITH
Try with rich fish and seafood dishes, or roast pork with apples or plums.

STYLE
Rich & Rounded White Wines

GRAPE VARIETY
Viognier

BACKSTORY
Les Vignerons Ardéchois is a large company, made up of 14 co-operatives and over 1,500 growers. It produces almost 60 million bottles of wine a year. Despite its size, it succeeds in making a series of sound reliable wines at keen prices, and one or two real gems, including the Viognier above. Viognier is not an easy grape to grow; there are plenty of wishy-washy versions around, but this is the real thing.

48

Marc Kreydenweiss Pinot Blanc Kritt 2014, Alsace
France 13% **€17.99** Organic

STOCKISTS: O'Briens

Marc Kreydenweiss Pinot Blanc Kritt 2014, Alsace

TASTING NOTE
A captivating wine with delicate exotic fruits topped off with a touch of honey.

DRINK WITH
A great aperitif wine, and wonderful with lightly spicy Asian prawns or chicken.

STYLE
Rich & Rounded White Wines

GRAPE VARIETY
Pinot Blanc

BACKSTORY
I hesitate to mention that this wine has a little residual sugar; most of us think we like only dry white wines. Yet this wine, with its delicate ripe fruit and refreshing acidity, is balanced perfectly by a slight touch of honey. The estate has been in the family since 1850, and, in1989, became one of the first in the region to start farming biodynamically.

49
**DMZ Chenin Blanc 2014,
DeMorgenzon,
Western Cape**
South Africa 14% **€18**

STOCKISTS: Red Island, Skerries; Baggot St Wines;
Blackrock Cellar; Corkscrew; Probus Wines; Morton's
Ranelagh; Deveney's Dundrum; Drinks Store, D7.

DMZ Chenin Blanc 2014, DeMorgenzon, Western Cape

TASTING NOTE
A superb wine brimming with rich peachy fruits backed up by a clean mineral acidity.

DRINK WITH
Perfect with barbecued or grilled fish and chicken.

STYLE
Rich & Rounded White Wines

GRAPE VARIETY
Chenin Blanc

BACKSTORY
Wendy and Hylton Appelbaum bought the Morgenzon (morning sun) in 2003. Winemaker Carl Van der Merve has quickly established the estate as one of the rising stars of Stellenbosch, with a growing reputation for some of the best Chenin Blanc in South Africa. The Maestro, a reserve blend of various varieties, recently won a prestigious trophy at the Decanter Wine Awards, and the Reserve Chenin a trophy at the International Wine Challenge. This is a name to search out.

50

Carmen Gran Reserva Chardonnay 2013, Casablanca Valley
Chile 13.5% **€19.95**

STOCKISTS: SuperValu; Greenacres Wexford; Sweeney's Glasnevin; 64wine Sandycove; The Vintry D6; O'Donovan's Cork.

Carmen Gran Reserva Chardonnay 2013, Casablanca Valley

TASTING NOTE
Impeccably balanced Chardonnay with ripe peach and quince fruits, a subtle toastiness and a long crisp dry finish.

DRINK WITH
Perfect with chicken or rich fish dishes.

STYLE
Rich & Rounded White Wines

GRAPE VARIETY
Chardonnay

BACKSTORY
The Casablanca Valley lies only a few kilometres from the Pacific Ocean. The cooling sea breezes and frequent fog moderate the climate, making it the perfect place for growing Pinot Noir, Sauvignon and Chardonnay. Chile is making increasingly good Chardonnay, and the Casa Real Gran Reserva is a perfect example; if this came from one of the other New World countries I suspect it would cost a lot more. I am getting a little tired of crisp dry Chardonnays with simple apple fruits. This style, with its plump, mouth-filling fruits, good balancing acidity, and barely perceptible oak, makes for a far more interesting, food-friendly glass of wine.

51 **Antão Vaz da Peceguina
2014, Herdade de Malandinha
Nova, VR Alentejano**
Portugal 13.5% **€19.95**

STOCKISTS: The Corkscrew, Chatham St; La Touche,
Greystones; Fresh Outlets; Donnybrook Fair.

Antão Vaz da Peceguina 2014, Herdade de Malandinha Nova, VR Alentejano

TASTING NOTE
Textured peaches, bananas and custard, with a good backbone of acidity – an interesting and very moreish wine.

DRINK WITH
Try it with seafood risotto or paella.

STYLE
Rich & Rounded White Wines

GRAPE VARIETY
Antão Vaz

BACKSTORY
The Alentejo is the big hot centre of Portugal. Temperatures rise up to the forties for much of the summer. A hot climate usually means red wines, but here in Alentejo, they have a few local white grape varieties that work amazingly well. Picked early, Antão Vaz (pronounced sort of like Anton Vash) produces delicious fruity whites. The Soares family run Herdade de Malhadinha Nova, a boutique hotel, restaurant and farm in the Alentejo. They rear black pigs, cattle and horses, and grow olives and vines. Luis Duarte, a much admired wine consultant, oversees the winemaking.

52 Grauburgunder 2013, Wagner Stempel, Rheinhessen
Germany 12.5% **€19.95**
Organic

STOCKISTS: Donnybrook Fair; The Corkscrew, Chatham Street

Grauburgunder 2013, Wagner Stempel, Rheinhessen

TASTING NOTE
Plump rounded melon and apple fruits with a hint of spice. Delectable wine.

DRINK WITH
A nice aperitif or with creamy Asian fish and chicken dishes.

STYLE
Rich & Rounded White Wines

GRAPE VARIETY
Pinot Gris

BACKSTORY
Grauburgunder is the same grape as Pinot Grigio, but makes a very different style of wine in Germany. Wagner Stempel is one of the great wine estates of Germany, producing a string of great wines, often with a very attractive opulent richness.

53

d'Arenberg Lucky Lizard Chardonnay 2012, Adelaide Hills
Australia 13.5% **€22**

STOCKISTS: Donnybrook Fair; Egans, Portlaoise; Martins, Fairview; The Corkscrew, Dublin 2; Parting Glass, Enniskerry; McEntee, Kells, Sweeney's, Glasnevin.

d'Arenberg Lucky Lizard Chardonnay 2012, Adelaide Hills

TASTING NOTE
Lightly oaked with an attractive creaminess and succulent tropical fruit underpinned by a cool acidity.

DRINK WITH
This would be good with sole, turbot or lobster with a buttery sauce.

STYLE
Rich & Rounded White Wines

GRAPE VARIETY
Chardonnay

BACKSTORY
Chester Osborne stands out in any crowd with his long flowing curly locks and dazzling shirts. Behind the razzmatazz, he is a great winemaker responsible for a string of excellent red and white wines. Along with his father, the legendary Darry, he has taken d'Arenberg to new heights.

54

**Domaine Larue Puligny-
Montrachet 1er cru
La Garenne 2013**
France   13%   **€49.50**

STOCKISTS: Le Caveau, Kilkenny; Green Man Wines,
Terenure.

Domaine Larue Puligny-Montrachet 1er cru La Garenne 2013

TASTING NOTE
A text-book white Burgundy out of the top drawer. Racy acidity, subtle oak, complex white fruits with a lovely clean structure and excellent length.

DRINK WITH
Black sole or salmon swimming in a buttery sauce.

STYLE
Rich & Rounded White Wines

GRAPE VARIETY
Chardonnay

BACKSTORY
White Burgundy is probably the world's greatest dry white wine, but it can be very annoyingly inconsistent. They are usually very expensive (beware cheap examples) but for a real treat it is worth breaking open the piggy bank. The 2010 vintage of this wine was exquisite; the 2013 is not quite there yet, but will, I suspect, improve further over the next year or two.

55

**F.X. Pichler Grüner
Veltliner Loibner
Loibenberg 2012, Wachau**
Austria 14% **€50**

STOCKISTS: Redmond's, Ranelagh; 64wine, Glasthule

F.X. Pichler Grüner Veltliner Loibner Loibenberg 2012, Wachau

TASTING NOTE

Gloriously rich and powerful wine with layers of textured honeyed marzipan and melon fruits, balanced nicely by a clean acidity and a slight spritz.

DRINK WITH

Salmon, scallops or lobster for a real treat.

STYLE

Rich & Rounded White Wines

GRAPE VARIETY

Grüner Veltliner

BACKSTORY

I know what you are thinking - has he gone mad picking a €50 wine from Austria? Taste the wine and I think you will agree it is worth the money. The Pichler family has long been recognised as one of the finest producers of Riesling and Grüner Veltliner in the Wachau and in Austria generally. The style here is very different to Brundlmayer, Eichinger and Steininger whose wines feature elsewhere in this book; Pichler wines are opulent and powerful, but always retain perfect balance. They also age for a decade or more.

LIGHT & ELEGANT
REDS

56

**Frunza Pinot Noir
2014, Romania**
Romania 12% **€9.99**

STOCKISTS: Independent
nationwide including The Vintry
Rathgar; Gibneys Malahide; Fresh;
Morton's, Ranelagh; Morton's,
Salthill; Higgins, Clonskeagh; Brady's
Shankill; Cheers @ Bakers Corner;
Grape & Grain @ Leopardstown Inn;
O'Donovan's Cork; Ardkeen Waterford; Next Door Stores.

Frunza Pinot Noir
2014, Romania

TASTING NOTE
Pale in colour, with light, fragrant, tangy plum fruits.
Finishes slightly off-dry.

DRINK WITH
Great party wine, served cool.

STYLE
Light & Elegant Reds

GRAPE VARIETY
Pinot Noir

BACKSTORY
I recently visited Romania and came across several
fantastic local grape varieties making some very
interesting wines. Sadly, most are not available in this
country (although members of The Wine Society should
look out for the wines of Prince Stirbey). Romania
also offers a host of well-made international varieties,
including this very decent well-priced Pinot Noir.

57

Frappato 2013, IGP Terre Siciliane
Italy 12% **€12.29**

STOCKISTS: Marks & Spencer

Frappato 2013, IGP
Terre Siciliane

TASTING NOTE
Light, fresh and delicate with scented squashed
strawberry fruits.

DRINK WITH
By itself, with antipasti and salumi, or with grilled fish as
the locals do.

STYLE
Light & Elegant Reds

GRAPE VARIETY
Frappato

BACKSTORY
Frappato is a local Sicilian variety with real potential.
The wines have these incredibly seductive, feather-light,
scented silky strawberry fruits. Last year I featured the
amazing COS Cerasuolo di Vitorria which includes 40%
Frappato in its makeup. The M&S version, made from
100% Frappato, is a delightful light summery glass of
wine, the sort of summery wine I drink all year round.

58

**Sangoiovese Rubicone
Medici Ermete,
Emilia-Romagna**
Italy 11.5% **€12.95**

STOCKISTS: Sheridans Cheesemongers, (Dublin, Galway &
Carnaross Co.Meath)

Sangoiovese Rubicone
Medici Ermete, Emilia-Romagna

TASTING NOTE
Low in alcohol and with no tannins, this is an irresistible wine with light, rounded, soft raspberry and red cherry fruits.

DRINK WITH
On its own or with light lunches.

STYLE
Light & Elegant Reds

GRAPE VARIETY
Sangiovese

BACKSTORY
Four generations of the Medici family have run this estate, regarded as one of the finest producers of Lambrusco, a much misunderstood wine. I fell in love with this one; completely unrecognisable as the Sangiovese made in Tuscany, this has a refreshing charm that is dangerously seductive.

59 **Caves Saint-Désirat
Syrah 2013 Vin de
pays d'Ardèche**
France 12% **€14.49**

STOCKISTS: O'Briens

Caves Saint-Désirat Syrah 2013 Vin de pays d'Ardèche

TASTING NOTE
Light, fresh, juicy peppery blackcurrant and damson fruits, with a mineral quality. You won't mistake it for a Côte Rôtie, but this is a great easy-drinking wine.

DRINK WITH
A good all-purpose red, especially with pork and charcuterie.

STYLE
Light & Elegant Reds

GRAPE VARIETY
Syrah

BACKSTORY
The Cave Saint-Désirat is a co-operative founded in 1960, based in St. Joseph, one of the appellations of the Northern Rhône. It is large, with control over 431 hectares of vines, and is responsible for 40% of all St. Joseph's production. The overall standard is very high. You will find their wines in various guises, usually at very keen prices.

60

Hacienda Lopez de Haro Rioja Crianza
Spain 13.5% **€14.50**

STOCKISTS: 64wine, Glasthule; Green Man Wines, Terenure; Jus de Vine, Portmarnock.

Hacienda Lopez de Haro Rioja Crianza

TASTING NOTE
Attractive light wine with subtle oak and pleasant red cherry and raspberry fruits. Great value too.

DRINK WITH
Lamb chops would be the local favourite, but pork chops would do nicely too.

STYLE
Light & Elegant Reds

GRAPE VARIETY
Tempranillo, Garnacha, Graciano

BACKSTORY
Wine lovers tend to concentrate on the reservas and gran reservas of Rioja. These may be great wines (although some are either over-oaked or made from inferior wine), but I have a soft spot for the jovens and crianzas - lightly oaked or unoaked wines that allow the fruit to shine through. They also cost a lot less! This particular wine is cracking value.

61

Anima Umbra 2012, Arnaldo Caprai, Umbria
Italy 12.5% **€14.50**

STOCKISTS: The Cheese Pantry, Dublin 9; Listons, Camden St.; 64Wine, Glasthule; Clontarf Wines; Redmonds, Ranelagh; Ennis South Circular Road; The Vineyard, Galway.

Anima Umbra 2012, Arnaldo Caprai, Umbria

TASTING NOTE
A very friendly wine with cool, linear, juicy dark fruits and light tannins. Great everyday wine at a bargain price.

DRINK WITH
This would be great with pork, roast chicken and lighter red meat dishes.

STYLE
Light & Elegant Reds

GRAPE VARIETY
Sangiovese, Canaiolo

BACKSTORY
Arnaldo Caprai is best-known for reviving the name of Montefalco di Sagrantino, a red wine made using the passito method (where grapes are partially dried on straw mats or pallets in order to concentrate flavour), and other specialities from the Montefaclo region in Umbria. This is a more 'normal' wine, made with the same varieties as grown in neighbouring Tuscany. I hadn't tasted it for a while and was very pleasantly surprised.

62

La Maldicíon Tinto para beber de Marc Isart 2014 D.O. Madrid
Spain 13.5% **€14.50**

STOCKISTS: 64wine, Glasthule

La Maldicíon Tinto para beber de Marc Isart 2014 D.O. Madrid

TASTING NOTE
Light, fresh and full of free-flowing juicy bouncy fruits with a smooth finish. A joy to drink.

DRINK WITH
One to try with medium-bodied meat dishes - it worked well with my chicken in a tomato sauce.

STYLE
Light & Elegant Reds

GRAPE VARIETY
Tempranillo, Malvar

BACKSTORY
Marc Isart looks after winemaking at Bodegas Bernabeleva, an estate that does wonderful things with Garnacha in the D.O. Madrid, south of the Spanish capital. This wine, from the same region, is made primarily with Tempranillo and a little of the white grape, Malvar, blended in to bring even more freshness to the party. Every now and again you come across a wine that puts a real smile on your face. This is certainly one. Great value for money.

63

Carmen Right Wave Leyda Valley Pinot Noir 2014
Chile 13.5% **€14.99**

STOCKISTS: Widely available including Dunnes Stores, SuperValu, Spar and Tesco.

Carmen Right Wave Leyda Valley Pinot Noir 2014

TASTING NOTE
Light, scented juicy raspberry and red cherry fruits; serve cool or even lightly chilled.

DRINK WITH
Perfect on its own, with salady lunches or seared tuna.

STYLE
Light & Elegant Reds

GRAPE VARIETY
Pinot Noir

BACKSTORY
The Leyda and Casablanca Valleys in Chile produce some seriously good Pinot Noir these days - and often at very good prices too. The cool Pacific temperatures have proven ideal for this famously fussy grape variety. Pinot Noir is never a big and tannic; more a ballerina than a prop? This wine also appeared in last year's book, but the 2014 vintage is even better.

64

Le Salare Montepulciano d'Abruzzo 2013
Italy 12.5% **€14.99**

STOCKISTS: La Touche,
Greystones; Sheridan's
Cheesemongers (Dublin,
Galway & Carnaross Co.Meath);
Lettercollum Kitchen Project,
Clonakilty; Ashe's, Annascaul, Co.Kerry; John
R's, Listowel.

Le Salare Montepulciano d'Abruzzo 2013

TASTING NOTE
Delicious, refreshing red wine with lifted aromas of roses and cherry, and a juicy palate of dark cherry fruits with mouth-watering acidity.

DRINK WITH
Try with pork and charcuterie

STYLE
Light & Elegant Reds

GRAPE VARIETY
Montepulciano

BACKSTORY
Montepulciano d'Abruzzo comes in many guises, including a great many poor quality wines and quite a few with too much oak. The best versions for me are light and refreshing with mouthwatering fruits; perfect quaffing wine and great with lighter foods. This is one of the good guys.

65

**Roka Blaufränkisch
2013, Stajerska**
Slovenia 12.5% **€15.99**

STOCKISTS: On the Grapevine, Dalkey (onthegrapevine.
ie); Cabot and Co, Westport (cabotandco.com); No.1 Pery
Square, Limerick; McCambridges, Galway.

Roka Blaufränkisch 2013, Stajerska

TASTING NOTE
Light, fragrant and seductive with free-flowing and refreshing pure dark cherry fruits.

DRINK WITH
This would be perfect for sipping with friends or served with tuna, salmon or cold meats.

STYLE
Light & Elegant Reds

GRAPE VARIETY
Blaufränkisch

BACKSTORY
An enterprising Irish couple, Sinéad and Liam Cabot, play tag-team winemaking, flitting between Slovenia and Westport, producing two appetising juicy red wines in one country, and running a wine business in the other. This is their very tasty entry-level wine; if you feel like splashing out, the Reserva at around €22 is even better.

66

Langhe Rosso 2013
Maretti
Italy 13.5% **€17.90**

STOCKISTS: 64wine, Glasthule; Green Man Wines, Terenure;
Jus de Vine, Portmarnock.

Langhe Rosso 2013 Maretti

TASTING NOTE
The Nebbiolo brings slightly austere savoury fruits, the
Barbera a juicy light touch; they come together to form
a medium-bodied wine with nicely balanced cool dark
fruits.

DRINK WITH
Mushroom risotto or meat ravioli.

STYLE
Light & Elegant Reds

GRAPE VARIETY
Barbera, Nebbiolo

BACKSTORY
Piemonte in north-western Italy is home to two of the
country's most famous names and greatest wines; Barolo
and Barbaresco. There is much more to discover in
the region though; scratch a little deeper and you will
discover the most wonderfully eclectic range of distinctive
and unique wines that go perfectly with the excellent
local cuisine.

67

J. Regnaudot
Bourgogne Pinot Noir
2013
France 12.5% **€18.25**

STOCKISTS: Le Caveau, Kilkenny; Baggot Street Wines; Blackrock Cellar; Corkscrew, Chatham Street; Donnybrook Fair; Fallon and Byrne; On the Grapevine Dalkey; Redmonds, Ranelagh; Listons, Camden St; MacGuinness Wines, Dundalk; 64 wines: Green Man Wines, Terenure.

J. Regnaudot Bourgogne Pinot Noir 2013

TASTING NOTE
Delightful fragrant Burgundy, with piquant cherry and wild hedgerow fruits. Unputdownable once you start.

DRINK WITH
Charcuterie, cold meats or seared salmon..

STYLE
Light & Elegant Reds

GRAPE VARIETY
Pinot Noir

BACKSTORY
Bourgogne Rouge from a good producer can be a bargain in Burgundian terms. This is a tiny region and demand is always high, so don't expect to find sub €10 bottles - if you do, be very suspicious! But good Bourgogne Rouge is a wonderful drink, refreshing and satisfying, great with or without food. I like to serve it at cool room temperature. I have enjoyed this particular wine several times throughout 2015.

68

**Bourgogne Pinot Noir
Les Tilles 2013,
Patrice Cacheux**
France 12.5% **€19.50**

STOCKISTS: La Touche, Greystones; Donnybrook Fair;
McCabes, Blackrock & Foxrock.

Bourgogne Pinot Noir Les Tilles 2013, Patrice Cacheux

TASTING NOTE
Lovely sweet cherry aromas, and delicate, but concentrated, cool fruits with good structure and length.

DRINK WITH
Roast pork, ham, grilled duck breast or game birds.

STYLE
Light & Elegant Reds

GRAPE VARIETY
Pinot Noir

BACKSTORY
The 2011 was the star wine in a tasting of less expensive red Burgundies earlier this year. The 2013 is every bit as good. I know €19.50 doesn't seem cheap, but red Burgundy really only starts at around €20 and then moves rapidly upwards! However, this is the true home of Pinot Noir, and I love the wines.

69

Castello di Verduna
Barbera d'Alba 2013
Italy 13.5% **€21.50**

147

STOCKISTS: Sheridans Cheesemongers (Dublin, Galway & Carnaross Co.Meath); Mitchell & Son, chq, Sandycove and Avoca, Kilmacanogue; Rua, Castelbar.

Castello di Verduna Barbera d'Alba 2013

TASTING NOTE
A textbook Barbera with real substance; concentrated tangy piquant blackcurrant fruits, good acidity and an earthy note.

DRINK WITH
Breast of duck or a plate of charcuterie.

STYLE
Light & Elegant Reds

GRAPE VARIETY
Barbera

BACKSTORY
Widely grown throughout Italy, Barbera is happiest in its home territory of Piemonte. It may not have the gravitas and ageing ability of Nebbiolo, but it does produce very satisfying wines with vivid fresh sweet/sour dark fruits that can be enjoyed young.

70

Moric Blaufränkisch 2012, Burgenland
Austria 13% €22.99

2012
**BLAU
FRÄNKISCH**
BURGENLAND
ÖSTERREICH QUALITÄTSWEIN TROCKEN
MIT STAATLICHER PRÜFNUMMER L-N 8305/13
PRODUZIERT UND ABGEFÜLLT VON ROLAND VELICH GMBH, A-7051 GROSSHÖFLEIN
ENTHÄLT SULFITE/CONTAINS SULFITES
WWW.MORIC.AT
13% VOL   750 ML
MORIC

STOCKISTS: On the Grapevine, Dalkey (onthegrapevine. ie); Cabot and Co, Westport (cabotandco.com); No.1 Pery Square, Limerick; McCambridges, Galway; 64wine, Glasthule; Morton's, Galway.

Moric Blaufränkisch 2012, Burgenland

TASTING NOTE
A delicious elegant light wine with piquant sour cherry, cranberry and blueberry fruits.

DRINK WITH
I have enjoyed it with roast chicken (always a good way to show off your wine) and roast pork.

STYLE
Light & Elegant Reds

GRAPE VARIETY
Blaufränkisch

BACKSTORY
As I wrote last year, this is one of my favourite wines. Roland Velich was one of those responsible for the current revival of interest in Blaufränkisch in Austria. His wines are refined and elegant, with a wonderful purity of fruit. He is not alone; there are now a number of Austrian producers making wines in a similar vein. I tend to avoid the more expensive versions, which often have lots of new oak, in favour of the fruit-filled entry-level wines.

71

**Muhr Van der Niepoort
Samt & Seide 2012,
Carnuntum**
Austria 13% **€23**

STOCKISTS: Greenacres, Wexford; Redmond's, Ranelagh;
Donnybrook Fair; Morton's of Galway; The Corkscrew,
Chatham St.; La Touche Wines, Greystoones.

Muhr Van der Niepoort Samt & Seide 2012, Carnuntum

TASTING NOTE
The name says it all - velvet and silk. Fragrant and delicate with piquant dark cherry fruits. A wine with real finesse.

DRINK WITH
Good with oily fish - trout, salmon and tuna, or with chicken and pork.

STYLE
Light & Elegant Reds

GRAPE VARIETY
Blaufränkisch

BACKSTORY
The name has changed slightly from last year, but the wine is every bit as good. Produced by Austrian PR guru Dorli Muhr in partnership with her ex-husband Dirk Niepoort, better known for some great wines from the Douro Valley in Portugal. Muhr aims for wines that are subtle and delicate with silky light fruits, and succeeds brilliantly.

72 Ziereisen Tschuppen 2012, Badischer Landwein
Germany 12.5% **€24**

153

STOCKISTS: 64 Wine, Glasthule; Redmond's, Ranelagh; Terroirs, Donnybrook; La Touche, Greystones; Bean and Berry, Wexford.

Ziereisen Tschuppen 2012, Badischer Landwein

TASTING NOTE
Lively fresh sour cherry and cranberry fruits, with earthy notes. Delightful subtle wine.

DRINK WITH
Ham or roast pork should work well.

STYLE
Light & Elegant Reds

GRAPE VARIETY
Pinot Noir

BACKSTORY
Several generations of the Ziereisen family run a large traditional farm in Baden in the south of Germany. There is a shop offering whatever is in season (they grow a lot of asparagus) and four guest rooms. Hanspeter looks after the wine and enjoys a reputation as one of Germany's finest winemakers. Last year I featured his wonderful pristine Chasselas; this year his Pinot Noir.

73

Ka Manciné Rossesse di Dolceacqua Bergana 2014
Italy 12.5% €26

STOCKISTS: The Corkscrew, Chatham St., D2: The Wicklow Wine Company, Wicklow Main Street

Ka Manciné Rossesse di Dolceacqua Bergana 2014

TASTING NOTE
Haunting, light, fragrant leafy aromas, soft crunchy red fruits and an elegant fresh finish. Sensational wine.

DRINK WITH
I would prefer to sip this slowly on its own, but I think something mild from the north of Italy - gnocchi with butter and parmesan? - would do nicely.

STYLE
Light & Elegant Reds

GRAPE VARIETY
Rossese

BACKSTORY
I tried this wine last year, and was blown away by the amazing ethereal silky fruit. It was the first and only time I had tried a wine made from the Rossesse grape. Sadly the importer, Wicklow Wine Company, had very little available so I couldn't include it in the 2015 edition. This year, they have better stocks. But don't leave it too late to visit their shop on Wicklow Main Street!

74

Fürst Spätburgunder Tradition 2011
Germany 13% **€29.95**

157

STOCKISTS: On the Grapevine, Dalkey; Cabot & Co., Westport; One Pery Square, Limerick; 64wine, Glasthule.

Fürst Spätburgunder Tradition 2011

TASTING NOTE
Fragrant and soft, developing some leafiness, with sweet, soft, dark cherry fruits.

DRINK WITH
Salmon, ham or roast duck.

STYLE
Light & Elegant Reds

GRAPE VARIETY
Pinot Noir

BACKSTORY
This featured last year, but it is amongst my favourite wines every year. I love German Pinot Noir, or Spätburgunder as it is known locally, and Fürst is one of the best in Germany. I have very happy memories of a visit to his cellars a few years ago. I even shelled out €50 for a bottle of one of his ethereal single-vineyard cuvées! But all of his wines, this one included, are scented and fragrant, with soft, silky fruits.

75

Greystone Pinot Noir 2012, Waipara
New Zealand 13.5% **€34**

STOCKISTS: Redmonds, Ranelagh; Clontarf Wines; Donnybrook Fair; DSix; La Touche, Greystones; Deveneys, Dundrum; Power, Lucan; Gibneys, Malahide; Thomas Woodberrys, Galway.

Greystone Pinot Noir 2012, Waipara

TASTING NOTE
A very seductive oak-kissed voluptuous style of Pinot, ripe with fleshy dark cherry fruits overlaid with woodsmoke.

DRINK WITH
Roast duck sounds very good.

STYLE
Light & Elegant Reds

GRAPE VARIETY
Pinot Noir

BACKSTORY
Marlborough, Martinborough and Central Otago in New Zealand have all built a reputation for making very good Pinot Noir. Waipara, just north of Christchurch, tends to get ignored. This is a pity, as the region makes some seriously good Chardonnay (the Greystone Chardonnay is worth checking out too) and equally good Pinot Noir. A visit to this beautiful region was one of the highlights of 2015 for me.

76

Nuits St. Georges 'Les Hauts Pruliers' 2010 Maison Ambroise
France 13% **€46.35**

STOCKISTS: Le Caveau, Kilkenny; Jus de Vine, Portmarnock; Green Man Wines, Terenure.

Nuits St. Georges 'Les Hauts Pruliers' 2010 Maison Ambroise

TASTING NOTE
Classic Nuits Saint Georges with firm dark cherry and blackcurrant fruits, hints of spice and a good long finish.

DRINK WITH
Roast duck, goose or any game bird.

STYLE
Light & Elegant Reds

GRAPE VARIETY
Pinot Noir

162

BACKSTORY
Red Burgundy is always in short supply, more so in recent years due to poor harvests combined with increased interest from consumers. I was delighted to come across this excellent wine. In Burgundian terms it represents something of a bargain. Good Nuits St. Georges has a satisfying firm meatiness and this wine has it in spades.

77

**La Penetencia 2013
Ribera Sacra**
Spain 13.5% **€50**
Organic

STOCKISTS: Jus de Vine, Portmarnock; Donnybrook Fair;
The Wine Store: thewinestore.ie; 64wine, Glasthule.

La Penetencia 2013
Ribera Sacra

TASTING NOTE
Elegant dark cherry and blueberry fruits on nose and palate. Piquant, poised and precise with fine tannins on a wonderful lingering finish.

DRINK WITH
Drink with pork dishes or duck and game, or hard cheeses.

STYLE
Light & Elegant Reds

GRAPE VARIETY
Mencía, Alicante Bouchet, Bastardo Caiño

BACKSTORY
I presented this wine at the Ballymaloe Litfest 2015 (see my blog at wilsononwine.ie), as representative of the exciting things happening in northwest Spain. The vines are planted on almost vertical ancient terraces. The entire area is hauntingly beautiful. La Pentencia is made by the region's most famous winemaker, Raúl Pérez. It is from a single vineyard with slate soils and hundred-year-old vines. The wine is expensive but enchanting and memorable.

78

**Ata Rangi Pinot Noir
2013, Martinborough**
New Zealand 13.5% **€63.99**

STOCKISTS: The Corkscrew, Dublin 2; O'Briens; On the
Grapevine, Dalkey; Thewineshop.ie; Green Man Wines,
Terenure.

Ata Rangi Pinot Noir 2013, Martinborough

TASTING NOTE
The 2013 is a stunning wine, structured and powerful, bursting with ripe dark fruits, hints of spice and a lingering long mineral finish.

DRINK WITH
A seared breast of duck or roast lamb.

STYLE
Light & Elegant Reds

GRAPE VARIETY
Pinot Noir

BACKSTORY
Ata Rangi is one of the pioneering estates of Martinborough in New Zealand. Run by Clive Paton, his wife Phyll and sister Ali with winemaking by Helen Masters, this is one of the best producers of Pinot in the country. They also make a stunning Chardonnay – check out the Craighall 2013 if you get the opportunity. The 2013 Pinot Noir is quite exceptional; I am already saving.

ROUNDED AND FRUITY RED WINES

79

**Aranleón Blés Tinto
2014, Valencia**
Spain 13.5% **€11**

STOCKISTS: Dunnes Stores

Aranleón Blés Tinto
2014 Valencia

TASTING NOTE
Nicely scented, with soft, easy pure plum fruits; supple and harmonious wine.

DRINK WITH
A great all-purpose everyday wine to drink on its own, or with grilled meats, pizza and most pasta dishes.

STYLE
Rounded & Fruity Red Wines

GRAPE VARIETY
Bobal

BACKSTORY
I've gone a little over the top on Bobal this year, with three entries. But I do love the wines, and really enjoyed a visit to the Aranleón stand at a wine fair earlier this year. If you are looking for fruity gluggable wines at bargain prices, look no further. Dunnes regularly promote this wine at €9.50 a bottle, when it becomes an even greater bargain.

80

Perricone Caruso e Minini 2013 Terre Siciliane IGT
Italy 14% **€12.29**

STOCKISTS: Marks & Spencer

Perricone Caruso e Minini 2013 Terre Siciliane IGT

TASTING NOTE
A pleasantly whacky wine bursting with sweet juicy ripe cherry and black fruits given extra interest by a nice herby edge. Very different, very enjoyable, and great value too.

DRINK WITH
Light enough to drink solo, but with enough body to match up nicely to spicy red meat dishes and pasta.

STYLE
Rounded & Fruity Red Wines

GRAPE VARIETY
Perricone

BACKSTORY
Perricone is a little-known native Sicilian grape variety. I had never tasted it before I came across this version from M&S, but I will certainly keep an eye out for it in future. Once simply a source of bulk table wine, Sicily is fast becoming one of the most exciting wine regions of Italy. There are three Sicilian wines in this book, all from M&S. Of all the supermarkets, Marks & Spencer tends to be the most adventurous. Recently this has meant wines from all over the Mediterranean, some of them really enjoyable.

81

Castro de Valtuille 2013
Bierzo
Spain 14% **€13.50**

173

STOCKISTS: The Black Pig, Donnybrook; Baggot Street
Wines; Red Island Wines, Skerries; Clontarf Wines; Blackrock
Cellar; Sweeney's, Glasnevin; 64wine, Glasthule; Fallon &
Byrne, Exchequer St.; Whelehan'ss, Loughlinstown.

Castro de Valtuille 2013 Bierzo

TASTING NOTE
Smooth, meaty savoury dark fruits in a wine that slips
down all too easily. One of the best value wines in the
market at the moment.

DRINK WITH
A very good all-purpose wine to serve alongside
medium-bodied meat, vegetarian and cheese dishes.

STYLE
Rounded & Fruity Red Wines

GRAPE VARIETY
Mencía

BACKSTORY
This featured in last year's book, and was also one of my
wines of the year in The Irish Times the previous year. I
like it! 2013 was not the easiest vintage in north-west
Spain, but this wine is a good as ever. It is made by one
of Spain's greatest winemakers, Raúl Pérez, who was
also responsible for the La Penetencia (see page 161).
Castro Ventosa, his family business, is one of the largest
producers in Bierzo, and also one of the very best.

82 **Aranleón Encuentro
2014, DOP Valencia**
Spain 13.4% **€13.99**
Organic

STOCKISTS: O'Briens

Aranleón Encuentro 2014, DOP Valencia

TASTING NOTE
Very moreish supple dark plum fruits with a sprinkle of spice. Excellent value for money.

DRINK WITH
A good all-purpose wine to serve with most meat and cheese dishes, so long as they aren't too big in flavour.

STYLE
Rounded & Fruity Red Wines

GRAPE VARIETY
Bobal

BACKSTORY
This is one of three wines made from Bobal in the book-you could do your own mini-Bobal tasting. It is a little-known variety planted in huge quantities in south-east Spain. Until recently it was mainly used for bulk wines and blending, but is now showing real potential. This is the big brother of the Blés, which is available in Dunnes Stores.

83

**Oveja Tinta 2014,
Bodegas Fontana**
Spain 13.5% **€13.99**

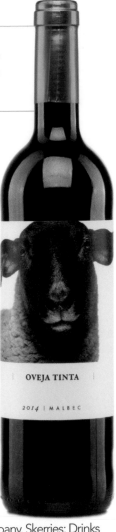

OVEJA TINTA

2014 | MALBEC

STOCKISTS: Red Island Wine Company, Skerries; Drinks Store, Manor Street; Martin's, Fairview; Mitchell & Son, CHQ, Glasthule and Avoca Kilmacanogue; Probus, Fenian Street; Blackrock Cellar.

Oveja Tinta 2014, Bodegas Fontana

TASTING NOTE
Aromatic with vibrant juicy dark fruits, and a rounded finish. Great everyday drinking.

DRINK WITH
Good with most white or red meats. Try it with your barbecue.

STYLE
Rounded & Fruity Red Wines

GRAPE VARIETY
Malbec

BACKSTORY
The label doesn't give much information, but it does come from Bodegas Fontana, a winery in Uclés, on the northern border of the vast La Mancha region. They make wines from both regions. I have always found the wines to be very well-made, with a freshness sometimes lacking in La Mancha, and generally very keenly priced. This wine is cracking value at €13.99.

84

Les Auzines Cuvée Hautes Terres 2011 Corbières
France 13.5% **€14.49**
Organic

STOCKISTS: O'Briens

Les Auzines Cuvée Hautes Terres 2011 Corbières

TASTING NOTE
Crunchy ripe blackcurrants with a herbal note and a clean lightly tannic finish.

DRINK WITH
Roast or grilled red meats.

STYLE
Rounded & Fruity Red Wines

GRAPE VARIETY
Carignan, Grenache, Syrah

BACKSTORY
Laurent Miquel and his Irish wife Neasa bought this beautiful estate high up in the mountains of Corbières a few years ago. Here they craft some delicious medium-bodied wines, both white and red, by organic methods. Miquel also makes a huge array of less expensive wines that you will find on our supermarket shelves - these are usually pretty good too.

85 **Valli Unite 'Ottavio Rube Rosso' 2013**
Italy 13.5% **€14.55**
Organic

OTTAVIO RUBE

VINO ROSSO

STOCKISTS: Le Caveau, Kilkenny; World Wide Wines, Waterford; Fallon and Byrne, Exchequer St.; Blackrock Cellar; Green Man Wines, Terenure.

Valli Unite 'Ottavio Rube Rosso' 2013

TASTING NOTE
Funky cool crunchy blackcurrant fruits with a nice tangy acidity; refreshing and interesting. By the next day it had softened, taking on very earthy flavours.

DRINK WITH
Salami, cold meats and cheese.

STYLE
Rounded & Fruity Red Wines

GRAPE VARIETY
Dolcetto, Barbera

BACKSTORY
Valli Unite is a co-operative, started 50 years ago by three idealistic farmers who pooled their land and resources to create a biodynamic farm. There are now 15 families involved in the business. This is a natural wine, biodynamic and made with little or no sulphur added. It certainly tastes different, but I really enjoyed it.

86 Haute Côt(e) de Fruit 2104, Fabien Jouves, Cahors
France 12.5% **€14.95**

Vin de Cahors

AUTE CÔT(E) DE FRUI

Malbec

FABIEN JOUVES

STOCKISTS: Terroirs, Donnybrook

Haute Côt(e) de Fruit 2104, Fabien Jouves, Cahors

TASTING NOTE
Right up my street. Light, fruity, unoaked with very attractive juicy dark fruits, a savoury twist. Delicious grown-up wine.

DRINK WITH
Pâtés & charcuterie or chicken dishes.

STYLE
Rounded & Fruity Red Wines

GRAPE VARIETY
Malbec

BACKSTORY
Cahors has a reputation for severe tannic wine that requires years in the cellar before you dare drink it. Modern Cahors is a very different animal, usually much more approachable. Some producers now make a younger fruitier style for early drinking, along with their more serious (and more expensive) wines. This is one such example.

87 Pegos Claros 2010, Palmela
Portugal 14% €14.99

STOCKISTS: La Touche, Greystones; Corkscrew, Chatham St.; O'Briens; O'Donovan's, Cork; Fresh; Donnybrook Fair; Fallon & Byrne, Exchequer St.; Deveney's, Dundrum & Rathmines; Redmonds,Ranelagh; Nectar, Sandyford; Sweeney's, Glasnevin; Mortons; The Coachouse,Ballinteer; The WineShop, Perrystown; Listons, Camden St.; Magic Carpet, Stillorgan; Mitchell & Son Glasthule, chq and Avoca, Kilmacanogue; Whelehan's Wines, Loughlinstown; Power & Co, Lucan; On The Grapevine, Dalkey; D Six; Red Island, Skerries; Mac Guinness Wines, Dundalk; Jus de Vine, Portmarnock; Drinks Store, D7; Baggot Street Wines.

Pegos Claros 2010, Palmela

TASTING NOTE
Bold and very beautiful wine; medium to full-bodied with a dangerously moreish palate of ripe liquorice, figs and dark fruits, finishing on a smooth note. Over-delivers at every stage.

DRINK WITH
I would go for red meat casserole or maybe a nice steak.

STYLE
Rounded & Fruity Red Wines

GRAPE VARIETY
Castelão

BACKSTORY
Palmela is a small region on the Setúbal peninsula, across the river Tagus from the capital Lisbon. In the sandy soils running right down to the Atlantic ocean the Castelão grape produces unique fruit-filled wines that can be drunk young, but have a cunning ability to age very well. The Pegos Claros is an old favourite that I hadn't tried for a year or two. I had forgotten just how good it is – great value wine.

88 La Malkerida 2012, Utiel-Requena
Spain 12.5% **€15.95**

STOCKISTS: Black Pig, Donnybrook; Michael's, Deerpark; Green Man Wines, Terenure; Power, Lucan; O'Learys, Cootehill; Quintessential, Drogheda www.quintessentialwines.ie

La Malkerida 2012, Utiel-Requena

TASTING NOTE
This is an engaging wine with delicious, plump, ripe, soft red fruits and light tannins. Very fairly-priced too.

DRINK WITH
A great all-purpose wine to sup with nibbles, or lighter vegetarian and meat dishes.

STYLE
Rounded & Fruity Red Wines

GRAPE VARIETY
Bobal

BACKSTORY
I featured the excellent Clos Lojen from Manchuela last year, but in the space of two months I came across several other excellent wines made from Bobal. This grape variety is the third most widely planted in Spain, but few wine drinkers have ever heard of it. Until recently it ended up in blends of inexpensive glugging wine. It deserves more than that, and over the last few years has really started to make a name for itself.

89

**7, rue de Pompe 2013,
Mas Coutelou,
Vin de France**
France 13.5% **€16.50**
Organic

STOCKISTS: 64wine, Glasthule; Green Man Wines, Terenure;
Jus de Vine, Portmarnock.

189

7, rue de Pompe 2013, Mas Coutelou, Vin de France

TASTING NOTE
Fascinating and utterly delicious wine. Fresh elegant cherry fruits with a distinct meatiness, a lovely intensity on the palate, good acidity and a clean finish.

DRINK WITH
A good all-rounder to serve with medium-bodied red and white meat dishes.

STYLE
Rounded & Fruity Red Wines

GRAPE VARIETY
Syrah, Grenache

BACKSTORY
Jean-Francois Coutelou was one of the earliest vignerons to convert to organic practices, way back in1987. He is now fully biodynamic. He has made quite a name for himself, despite releasing small quantities of a few wines each year, some of these under the lowly Vin de France category. He releases different cuvées; the grape varieties and winemaking methods vary according to the vintage. The wines are made with very little and sometimes no sulphur. If this is natural wine I want more!

90

Côtes du Rhône Les Deux Cols, Cuvée d'Alizé 2014
France 13.5% **€16.95**

STOCKISTS: 64wine, Glasthule; Donnybrook Fair; Jus de Vine, Portmarnock; One Pery Square, Limerick; The Drink Store, D7.

Côtes du Rhône Les Deux Cols, Cuvée d'Alizé 2014

TASTING NOTE
Delectable just-ripe dark fruits, with prefect balance and a smooth palate. An attractive medium-bodied wine that will develop over the coming year.

DRINK WITH
I would drink this with all manner of white and red meats, game and firm cheeses.

STYLE
Rounded & Fruity Red Wines

GRAPE VARIETY
Grenacha, Syrah, Cinsault

BACKSTORY
A new vintage of a wine produced by Irishman Simon Tyrrell, who also makes Craigie's Cider in this country. This is no ordinary Côtes du Rhône, but a very nicely crafted wine with excellent purity of fruit and a lovely freshness.

91

Tenute Dettori Vino Renosu Rosso NV
Italy 13% **€17.50**

193

Tenute Dettori Vino Renosu Rosso NV

TASTING NOTE
Warm, rounded, earthy and herby, with soft, plush, ripe red fruits – yet it still has a real elegance. Fascinating and delicious wine that was just as good the following evening.

DRINK WITH
Italian sausages with lentils or beans

STYLE
Rounded & Fruity Red Wines

GRAPE VARIETY
Cannonau

BACKSTORY
Allessandro Dettori, based on the island of Sardinia, is committed to non-interventionist natural wine making, using organic grapes, wild yeasts, ageing in cement tanks and as little sulphur dioxide as possible. His wines are certainly very different. I found them intriguing and delicious. If you are feeling flush, try his wonderful Ottomarzo 2012 (€29.50 in 64wine).

92 **Ch. Sainte-Marie Alios**
2012 Côtes de Bordeaux
France 13.5% **€17.95**

STOCKISTS: Wines Direct, Mullingar, winesdirect.ie

Ch. Sainte-Marie Alios
2012 Côtes de Bordeaux

TASTING NOTE
From a classic blend of Merlot, Cabernet and Petit
Verdot, a supple ripe wine filled with lightly spiced
blackcurrant and cassis.

DRINK WITH
A Sunday roast of lamb would be good.

STYLE
Rounded & Fruity Red Wines

GRAPE VARIETY
Merlot, Cabernet Sauvignon, Petiti Verdot.

BACKSTORY
Stephane Dupuch at Ch. Sainte-Marie, in the lowly Entre-
Deux-Mers appellation of Bordeaux, produces cracking
wines, full of modern ripe fruit, but with a little traditional
Bordelais restraint as well. I recommended one of his other
wines last year as well, but then I cannot remember ever
having tasted anything but good wine from this stable.

93

**Artuke Pies Negros
2013 Rioja**
Spain 14% **€18.90**

STOCKISTS: 64Wine, Glasthule; Clontarf Wines; Redmonds, Ranelagh; Ennis Butchers, South Circular Rd.; The Wicklow Wine Co; The Black Pig, Donnybrook.

Artuke Pies Negros 2013 Rioja

TASTING NOTE
A very nicely weighted palate of soft ripe raspberry
fruits, with a vibrant   freshness running throughout, and
a rounded finish.

DRINK WITH
Red meats with mushroom sauces

STYLE
Rounded & Fruity Red Wines

198

GRAPE VARIETY
Tempranillo, Graciano

BACKSTORY
The grapes for this wine are partly crushed by foot (clean
feet we hope!) before being fermented with some berries
still whole. This gives the wine a vibrant fruitiness, rounded
texture and soft finish. An atypical Rioja, but very enjoyable.

94
Domaine Eian da Ros Abouriou, Côtes du Marmandais 2012
France 12.5% **€19.50**
Organic

STOCKISTS: Terroirs, Donnybrook

Domaine Eian da Ros Abouriou, Côtes du Marmandais 2012

TASTING NOTE
Fabulous pure dark plum fruits layered with spice and dark chocolate, plus an underlying earthiness.

DRINK WITH
Roast or grilled lamb.

STYLE
Rounded & Fruity Red Wines

GRAPE VARIETY
Abouriou

BACKSTORY
Little-known outside (or indeed inside) of the Côtes du Marmandais, Abouriou here produces a unique and delicious wine. Elian da Ros is one hugely talented winemaker, who learned his craft working with Olivier Humbrecht in the famous Zind-Humbrecht estate in Alsace. He farms biodynamically, producing individual wines that combine a wonderful elegance with real concentration.

95
Il Molino di Grace 2012
Chianti Classico
Italy 13.5% **€19.95**

STOCKISTS: Whelehan's Wines, Loughlinstown

Il Molino di Grace 2012 Chianti Classico

TASTING NOTE
I wrote about the 2010 in The Irish Times earlier this year.
The follow-up 2012 is equally good. Classic juicy tart
cherries and herbs with well-judged tannins and a nice
snappy finish. Very pleasant harmonious wine.

DRINK WITH
A good match for pork dishes.

STYLE
Rounded & Fruity Red Wines

GRAPE VARIETY
Sangiovese, Canaiolo

BACKSTORY
Classic Chianti is a food wine; it has noticeable acidity
and drying tannins, possibly a little austere when drunk
on its own. But with a plate of grilled red meat or game, it
transforms into one of the world's great wines.

96

**Monte da Peceguina
Red 2013, Herdade de
Malhadinha Nova**
Portugal 13% **€20.95**

Monte da Peceguina
vinho regional alentejano · 2013
produzido e engarrafado na propriedade

Herdade da Malhadinha Nova
Albernôa · Portugal

STOCKISTS: La Touche,
Greystones; The Corkscrew,
Chatham St; Fresh Outlets;
O'Donovans, Cork; Donnybrook
Fair; Deveney's, Dundrum &
Rathmines; Fallon & Byrne;
Sweeney's; Nectar; Redmonds;
Mortons,; D Six; Listons; Whelehan's Wines; Red Island; Power
& Co; On The Grapevine; Baggot St. Wines; Green Man
Wines, Terenure; Mitchell & Son; The Wine Shop, Perrystown.

Monte da Peceguina Red 2013, Herdade de Malhadinha Nova

TASTING NOTE
A very moreish wine with plenty of smooth fresh strawberry fruits and an easy finish.

DRINK WITH
Chicken and pork dishes.

STYLE
Rounded & Fruity Red Wines

GRAPE VARIETY
Alicante Bouschet, Touriga Nacional, Cabernet Sauvignon

BACKSTORY
Regular travellers to the Algarve may be familiar with the Malandinha labels. Brothers Joao and Paulo Soares, along with their families, own a chain of 15 wine shops in the south; not surprisingly their wines feature alongside other Portuguese and foreign wines. When I met Joao and Rita Soares they were still enjoying the afterglow of several major awards for their wines. The estate is quite beautiful, set in the rolling hills, with a boutique hotel and restaurant. They produce their own olive oil, and rear black pigs, horses, and Alentejo cattle. The excellent claret-like Malandinha is also worth seeking out for a treat.

97 Astrolabe Pinot Noir
2010, Marlborough
New Zealand 14% **€25.49**

STOCKISTS: O'Briens

Astrolabe Pinot Noir 2010, Marlborough

TASTING NOTE
Enchanting, maturing, plush sweet dark cherry fruits with a subtle leafiness.

DRINK WITH
Perfect with game dishes.

STYLE
Rounded and Fruity Reds

GRAPE VARIETY
Pinot Noir

BACKSTORY
I am not generally a fan of Marlborough Pinot Noir – give me Martinborough, Central Otago or Waipara any day. Looking back at my notes, I wasn't hugely impressed by this wine two years ago either. Now it appears to have turned a corner; alongside a mushroom risotto, it was excellent.

98

Villa di Capezzana Carmignano 2011
Italy 15% **€34.99**

STOCKISTS: 64wine, Glasthule; Fallon & Byrne, Exhcequer St.; Green Man Wines, Terenure; Redmond's, Ranelagh; Jus de Vine, Portmarnock; Michael's, Deerpark; Red Island Wines, Skerries; Searsons, Monkstown.

Villa di Capezzana
Carmignano 2011

TASTING NOTE
A lovely spicy nose leads on to a seductive palate of soft and sweet red cherry fruits with hints of liquorice and a gently lingering finish.

DRINK WITH
Grilled or roast pork and veal.

STYLE
Rounded & Fruity Red Wines

GRAPE VARIETY
Sangiovese, Cabernet Sauvignon

BACKSTORY
Not many wineries can claim 12 centuries of production, but Villa di Capezzana proudly display a document from 804 that mentions vineyards and olive groves. They still produce both (the olive oil is superb too). Carmignano has a long history of growing Cabernet Sauvignon and up to 20% is permitted in the blend.

99 **Santa Rita Casa Real
2011, Maipo Valley**
Chile 14% **€49.95**

STOCKISTS: Redmond's, Ranelagh, The Loop, Dublin
Airport; The Corkscrew, Chatham St.

Santa Rita Casa Real 2011, Maipo Valley

TASTING NOTE
Discreet but intense flavours of cassis, blackcurrant and plums, with subtle oak and a long, firm, structured finish.

DRINK WITH
A roast leg of lamb with all the trimmings.

STYLE
Rounded & Fruity Red Wines

GRAPE VARIETY
Cabernet Sauvignon

BACKSTORY
The Alto Maipo Valley in Chile produces some of the world's finest Cabernet Sauvignon. Chileans delight in putting them into blind tastings alongside the great (and much more expensive) wines of Bordeaux and California. The results invariably put a few noses out of joint! Casa Real is one of the oldest and best of these Cabernets. I enjoyed a fantastic vertical tasting of ten vintages of Casa Real this year – all were still very much alive.

100

**Tolpuddle Vineyard Pinot
Noir 2013, Tasmania**
Australia 12.5% **€59.99**

STOCKISTS: 64wine, Glasthule; Green Man Wines, Terenure;
Redmond's, Ranelagh; Jus de Vine, Portmarnock.

Tolpuddle Vineyard Pinot Noir 2013, Tasmania

TASTING NOTE
Bright and subtle red cherries with a light spiciness, a vivid fresh quality and a mineral streak. Supremely elegant precise wine.

DRINK WITH
Something light - sea bass with herbs or salmon

STYLE
Rounded & Fruity Red Wines

GRAPE VARIETY
Pinot Noir

BACKSTORY
A decade ago, Tasmanian Pinot Noir tended to be a little bit too lean and green, but it has improved in leaps and bounds recently. On a trip there two years ago, I tasted some stunning wines. I wasn't surprised to see that this wine picked up a number of very prestigious awards. It is made by cousins Martin Shaw and Michael Hill Smith, who head up a highly-regarded eponymous winery on the mainland in Adelaide.

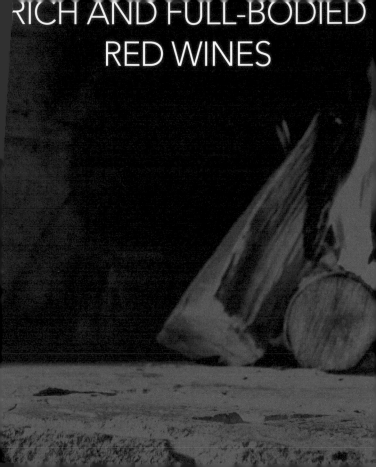

RICH AND FULL-BODIED
RED WINES

101

Porta 6 2012 Lisboa
Portugal 13.5% **€12.99**

STOCKISTS: O'Briens

Porta 6 2012 Lisboa

TASTING NOTE
Rounded ripe plum and blackberry fruits. A very gluggable crowd-pleaser.

DRINK WITH
This went very well with a roast shoulder of lamb, but beef would be good too.

STYLE
Rich & Full-bodied Red Wines

GRAPE VARIETY
Tinta Roriz, Castelão and Touriga Nacional.

BACKSTORY
The natty label features one of the historic trams that run around the streets of Portugal's capital city. António Mendes Lopes of Vidigal had bought the picture, but had great trouble tracking down the artist to get permission to use it on a label – it turned out to be a slightly eccentric German artist by the name of Hauke Vagt, who sold his works to tourists during the summer months. O'Briens offer this wine at €9.99 several times a year, when it becomes one of the best value wines around.

102 Pascual Toso Malbec
2013, Mendoza
Argentina 14% **€13.99**

STOCKISTS: Jus de Vine, Portmarnock; O'Donovans, Cork; 64wine, Glasthule; Thomas's, Foxrock; McCabes, Blackrock & Foxrock; World Wide Wines, Waterford; Drink Store, Manor St; The Wine Centre, Kilkenny; Egan's, Portlaoise; Redmonds, Ranelagh; Sweeney's, Glasnevin; Greenacres, Wexford; Power's, Lucan.

Pascual Toso Malbec 2013, Mendoza

TASTING NOTE
Medium to full-bodied with ripe dark loganberry fruits, good concentration and a nice dry finish. Great value for money.

DRINK WITH
Red meats, roast, grilled or stewed.

STYLE
Rich and Full-bodied Red Wines

GRAPE VARIETY
Malbec

BACKSTORY
The whole world wants Malbec at the moment, although I reckon Argentina makes some pretty tasty Cabernet as well. I have been a fan of the Pascual Toso Malbec for many years. It is consistent and very reasonably priced, despite the dollar-euro exchange rate.

103

Rafael Cambra El Bon Homme 2014, Valencia
Italy 13% €14

STOCKISTS: Blackrock Cellar; Fallon & Byrne; Baggot St Wines; Green Man Wines, Terenure; Black Pig, Donnybrook; 64Wine, Glasthule; Red Island Wines, Skerries; Redmonds, Ranelagh.

Rafael Cambra El Bon Homme 2014, Valencia

TASTING NOTE
Soft, supple juicy red wine with savoury dark plum fruits; medium to full-bodied with plenty of stuffing.

DRINK WITH
One to serve with warming stews and casseroles, or maybe lasagne.

STYLE
Rich & Full-bodied Red Wines

GRAPE VARIETY
Monastrell, Cabernet Sauvignon

BACKSTORY
The friendly face of Monastrell? This grape, known as Mourvèdre in France, and Mataro in Australia and California, is not the easiest variety to grow, and the wines can be equally challenging. On its home territory of South-East Spain - Jumilla, Alicante and Valencia - it produces wines that can be very high in alcohol and loaded with tannins. It takes a skilled winemaker, such as Rafael Cambra, to tame these tendencies. Here it is blended with Cabernet Sauvignon to produce a hugely drinkable, great value wine.

104

Libido 2013 Navarra, David Sampedro Gil
Spain 13.5% **€14.50**

221

LIBIDO
by DOG
100% GARNACHA
OLD VINES

NAVARRA
DENOMINACIÓN DE ORIGEN

STOCKISTS: Quintessential Wines, Drogheda
www.quintessentialwines.ie

Libido 2013 Navarra, David Sampedro Gil

TASTING NOTE
Lively, juicy ripe strawberry and raspberry fruits with an inviting gluggable quality.

DRINK WITH
A good pizza and pasta wine.

STYLE
Rich & Full-bodied Red Wines

GRAPE VARIETY
Garnacha

BACKSTORY
Great name for a wine, but we make no promises! David Sampedro Gil is a young winemaker from the Rioja region. As well as some excellent (but quite expensive) wines from Rioja, he makes this delicious wine from neighbouring Navarra. Made without any oak influence, it is full of youthful, exuberant Garnacha fruit.

105

**Dom Rafael 2012,
Mouchâo, Alentejo**
Portugal 13.5% **€14.50**

STOCKISTS: Clontarf Wines;
Wicklow Wine Co.; 64 Wine,
Glasthule; Jus de Vine, Portmarnock;
Martin's, Fairview; Probus Wines,
Fenian St; The Pig & Heifer; On the
Grapevine, Dalkey; Redmond's, Ranelagh; Hole in the Wall,
D7; Searsons, Monkstown.

Dom Rafael 2012, Mouchâo, Alentejo

TASTING NOTE
Lovely rich smooth red fruits, an earthy touch, plenty of power and well-integrated tannins on the finish.

DRINK WITH
Decant before serving and enjoy with substantial red meat dishes.

STYLE
Rich & Full-bodied Red Wines

GRAPE VARIETY
Alicante Bouschet, Aragonez, Trincadeira

BACKSTORY
Herdade de Mouchâo is one of the legendary estates of Portugal. Founded by the English Reynolds family in the 19th century, it has survived the baking hot Alentejo climate as well as the 1974 revolution in Portugal when local activists took over the winery and drank all of the wine. Today it produces the deeply-coloured tannic flagship Mouchâo wine, and Dom Rafael, the excellent second wine of the estate.

106

**Jean Bousquet
Cabernet Sauvignon
2013, Tupungato Valley**
Argentina 14.5% **€15.50**
Organic

STOCKISTS: Next Door, Kimmage; Bradleys, Cork; Nolans, Clontarf; Dalys, Boyle; Donnybrook Fair; World Wide Wines, Waterford; The Wine Centre, Kilkenny; 1601, Kinsale.

Jean Bousquet Cabernet Sauvignon 2013, Tupungato Valley

TASTING NOTE
Certainly not shy, this is a big, rich, swarthy Cab with tasty ripe cassis fruits overlaid with spice.

DRINK WITH
Beef, grilled or roast, would do very nicely.

STYLE
Rich & Full-bodied Red Wines

GRAPE VARIETY
Cabernet Sauvignon

BACKSTORY
Frenchman Jean Bousquet headed over to Argentina in 1990 to found a winery in the Tupungato Valley. With vineyards at an altitude of 1,200 metres, he benefits from cooler night-time temperatures. The organic wines are a tantalising, lipsmacking, mix of ripe fruit and good acidity.

107

Le Vin d'Adrien 2014
Domaine de l'Amauve
Côtes du Rhône
France 14.5% **€15.95**

STOCKISTS: Whelehan's Wines, Loughlinstown

Le Vin d'Adrien 2014 Domaine de l'Amauve Côtes du Rhône

TASTING NOTE

Big, rich, powerful wine with delicious rounded sweet strawberries and other red fruits. Beats many Châteauneuf-du-Pape at half the price.

DRINK WITH

This would go nicely with roast red meats and hearty casseroles.

STYLE

Rich & Full-bodied Red Wines

GRAPE VARIETY

Grenache, Syrah, Carignan

BACKSTORY

This estate, in the village of Séguret, is owned by Christian Voeux and his family. M. Vouex is a respected oenologist, who worked at Ch. Mont-Redon, one of the best estates in Châteauneuf-du-Pape, for 25 years. He now advises Ch. La Nerthe, another top estate in Châteauneuf-du-Pape. However, he still finds time to craft some excellent wines in his own domaine. Not surprisingly, they have something of the character and style of their better-known neighbour, but at a more interesting price.

108 Doña Paula Estate Malbec 2014, Uco Valley
Argentina 14% **€15.99**

STOCKISTS: Widely available, including O'Briens, SuperValu and Tesco.

Doña Paula Estate Malbec 2014, Uco Valley

TASTING NOTE
Listed last year as well, this is a very well-mannered and well-balanced Malbec with rich plush loganberry fruits, subtle vanilla spice, and plenty of power too.

DRINK WITH
Steak works really well, but I have enjoyed this with a wide variety of red and white meats.

STYLE
Rich & Full-bodied Red Wines

GRAPE VARIETY
Malbec

BACKSTORY
Malbec was imported by French immigrants to Argentina over a century ago. It has become Argentina's flagship wine, popular the world over. Deep in colour, Malbec grown in cooler climates, such as the Uco Valley, offers a dangerously moreish combination of power and juiciness.

109 Côtes du Rhône 2013, Domaine Saint Gayan
France 14% €16.95

STOCKISTS: Searsons Wine Merchants, Monkstown; Next Door, Ballyshannon.

Côtes du Rhône 2013, Domaine Saint Gayan

TASTING NOTE
This is a young wine with real concentration and length; never too big or alcoholic, but full-bodied with masses of dark fruits and liquorice. Worth every penny.

DRINK WITH
Warming winter stews or roast venison

STYLE
Rich & Full-bodied Red Wines

GRAPE VARIETY
Grenache, Syrah, Mourvèdre

BACKSTORY
Côtes du Rhône comes in all shapes and sizes; this vast area produces huge quantities of inexpensive glugging wine at very cheap prices. The more ambitious producers aim to make far better wines with real character, and charge a little more. The best wines offer great value. Domaine St Gayan, with vineyards in the posher areas of Rasteau, Sablet and Châteauneuf-du-Pape, is one such producer.

110 Ribeo 2011, Morellino di Scansano, Roccapesta
Italy 14% **€18.99**

233

STOCKISTS: Wines on the Green; Jus de Vine, Portmarnock; McCabes, Foxrock & Blackrock; 64wine, Glasthule

Ribeo 2011, Morellino di Scansano, Roccapesta

TASTING NOTE
Rounded and full-bodied, with soft cassis and a herbal note.

DRINK WITH
Drink with roast game birds, venison and beef.

STYLE
Rich & Full-bodied Red Wines

GRAPE VARIETY
Sangiovese, Alicante Bouschet

BACKSTORY
Morellino is a clone of Sangiovese grown in the Scansano region of Tuscany. It is part of Maremma, a region that became famous and fashionable through Sassicaia, one of Italy's most sought-after wines. Scansano runs up the hills from the Mediterranean coast. The wines here tend to be riper and fleshier than others produced further inland.

111
**Celler Lafou El Sender
2013 Terra Alta**
Spain 14% **€19.95**

STOCKISTS: Mitchell & Son, IFSC, Sandycove and Avoca, Kilmacanogue; Deveney's, Dundrum. Celler Lafou El Sender 2013 Terra Alta.

Celler Lafou El Sender
2013 Terra Alta

TASTING NOTE
Delicious and sophisticated, overflowing with plump sweet strawberries and a touch of tangy liquorice. Full-bodied yet fresh.

DRINK WITH
Something substantial - a rare grilled steak?

STYLE
Rich & Full-bodied Red Wines

GRAPE VARIETY
Garnacha, Syrah, Morenillo

BACKSTORY
Terra Alta is a small region high in the mountains south-east of Barcelona. Most of the wines here are made and sold through the co-operatives, and much of that is used as base wine to make Cava, the Catalan sparkling wine. However, there are now almost 50 smaller producers as well, many of them making very promising red wines that have developed a following amongst those in the know. The Lafou El Sender is one such wine.

112

Gaia S 2010, Koutsi Hillside Vineyard, Peleponnisos
Greece 14% **€23.49**

STOCKISTS: O'Briens

Gaia S 2010, Koutsi Hillside Vineyard, Peleponnisos, Greece

TASTING NOTE
This is a lovely mature wine; sweet ripe red fruits with a lovely savoury kick from the Syrah; full-bodied and rounded with good length.

DRINK WITH
Simple grilled meats; lamb chops or maybe pork.

STYLE
Rich & Full-bodied Red Wines

GRAPE VARIETY
Agiorgtiko, Syrah

BACKSTORY
I am a big fan of Gaia and of Greek wines in general. Any country with wines called Lesbos and Drama deserves our attention. With a history of winemaking going back 4,500 years and 300 indigenous grape varieties, the country should be sweeping all before it. Somehow it hasn't quite happened yet, but if it does, I am sure that guys like the amiable professorial Yannis Paraskevopoulos of Gaia will have played a large part in that success. Their other winery on Santorini produces a superb white Assyrtiko.

113

**Quellu' Cinsault
2013 Louis-Antoine
Luyt, Curico Valley**
Chile 14% **€23.90**

239

STOCKISTS: Le Caveau, Kilkenny; Green Man Wines,
Terenure; 64wine, Glasthule.

Quellu' Cinsault 2013
Louis-Antoine Luyt, Curico Valley

TASTING NOTE
Refreshing and leafy with redcurrant and tart cherry fruits.

DRINK WITH
Drink on its own, or with white meats.

STYLE
Rich & Full-bodied Red Wines

GRAPE VARIETY
Cinsault

BACKSTORY
Sommelier turned vigneron, Burgundian Louis-Antoine Luyt makes natural wines from his ancient (some 200 years old) vines in Chile. Made with natural yeasts, unfiltered and unfined, the wines are completely different to the standard Chilean fare. They will divide opinion but I loved this Cinsault.

114

Bodega Colomé Estate 2012, Cafayate
Argentina 14.5% **€24.99**

STOCKISTS: Blackrock Cellar; Clontarf Wines; Deveney's, Dundrum; Donnybrook Fair; Fallon & Byrne, Exchequer St.; Redmond's, Ranelagh; Jus de Vine, Portmarnock; Mitchell & Son, IFSC, Glasthule, Avoca Kilmacanogue; Green Man Wines, Terenure, The Corkscrew, Chatham St.; Thomas Woodberry, Galway.

Bodega Colomé Estate 2012, Cafayate

TASTING NOTE
Rippling with firm, concentrated, sweet/sour
blackcurrant fruits, finishing with some firm dry tannins.
Superb wine.

DRINK WITH
Red meat, grilled or roast would do very nicely.

STYLE
Rich & Full-bodied Red Wines

GRAPE VARIETY
Malbec

BACKSTORY
This wine also appeared in last year's book, but as one
of my favourite wines, that is hardly surprising. It was the
standout wine at a tasting of Argentinian Malbecs during
the year. Bodegas Colomé, founded in 1831, claims to
have the highest vineyards in the world, at over 3,000
metres. This unique climate produces wines that are
perfectly ripe, fresh and structured all at the same time.

115

Sijnn Red 2010
South Africa 14.5%
€27.90 Organic

STOCKISTS: Kinnegarwines.com; Mitchell & Son, ifsc, Glasthule and Avoca, Powerscourt.

Sijnn Red 2010

TASTING NOTE
Wild dark fruits on nose and palate; perfectly ripe with
a strong mineral element. Refreshing, smooth and
powerful with very good dry length. A very impressive
wine that evolves in the glass.

DRINK WITH
This calls for robust fare; roast or grilled red meats, or a
rich casserole.

STYLE
Rich & Full-bodied Red Wines

GRAPE VARIETY
Syrah, Tourgia Nacional, Mourvèdre, Trincadeira,
Cabernet.

BACKSTORY
David Trafford established de Trafford as one of the finest
producers in Stellenbosch before buying some new
vineyards in uncharted territory a few kilometres from the
coast. Here he makes a series of excellent wines under the
Sijnn (pronounced sane) label.

116

Ridge East Bench Zinfandel 2013, Dry Creek Valley, Sonoma County, California

USA 14.5% **£21.50/€29.95**

RIDGE 2013
EAST BENCH
ZINFANDEL

DRY CREEK VALLEY   100% ZINFANDEL
SONOMA COUNTY
GROWN, PRODUCED & BOTTLED BY RIDGE VINEYARDS
LYTTON SPRINGS RD, HEALDSBURG, CALIF 95448 USA
WINE OF U.S.A. 750 mL ALC. 14.5% VOL
CONTAINS SULPHITES

STOCKISTS: jnwine.com; Blackrock Cellars, Blackrock; The Counter Letterkenny; Whelehan's's, Loughlinstown.

Ridge East Bench Zinfandel 2013, Dry Creek Valley, Sonoma County, California

TASTING NOTE
As powerful as it is balanced, full of dense, alluring, plush dark fruits and a subtle note of spice.

DRINK WITH
One to serve with red meats; a well-hung steak would be ideal.

STYLE
Rich & Full-bodied Red Wines

GRAPE VARIETY
Zinfandel

BACKSTORY
For many years, Ridge has been my favourite Californian producer. Paul Draper and his team produce a string of wines laden with superb, complex ripe fruits. They always have a balance and subtlety lacking in many other far more expensive Californian wines. Memories of a tasting earlier this year of the stunning Ridge Monte Bello will remain for years to come.

117

Ch. Musar 2007, Bekaa Valley
Lebannon 14% €36.99

STOCKISTS: Molloy's Liquor Stores; SuperValu; The Corkscrew, Chatham St.; O'Driscoll's, Ballinlough; Chillin', Ongar; Joyce, Knocknacarra; Baggot St. Wines; Bradleys, Cork; Mitchell & Son, chq, Sandycove & Avoca, Kilmacanogue.

Ch. Musar 2007, Bekaa Valley

TASTING NOTE
A fascinating mix of leather, earthy spice and sweet baked mature red fruits. Smooth, full-bodied, beguiling and quite unlike any other wine.

DRINK WITH
I had mine with Lebanese-style spicy roast lamb.

STYLE
Rich & Full-bodied Red Wines

GRAPE VARIETY
Cabernet Sauvignon, Carignan, Cinsault

BACKSTORY
The vines were planted by Gaston Hochar in the Bekaa Valley back in 1930. His son Serge took over on his death and produced wine in virtually every vintage since, despite the wars and invasions that have beset Lebanon. Sadly Serge died at the start of 2015. His sons, Gaston and Marc, now run the show.

118

Casa Emma Chianti Classico Riserva 2010
Italy 14.5% **€39.95**

STOCKISTS: World Wide Wines, Waterford; Thomas Woodberry's, Galway; Wicklow Wine Co; On The Grapevine, Dalkey; The Corkscrew @ Kenny's Lucan; The Corkscrew Chatham St.

Casa Emma Chianti Classico Riserva 2010

TASTING NOTE
Very nicely balanced wine with meaty rich dark cherry fruits, good acidity and smooth tannins on the finish. Big but beautiful.

DRINK WITH
Hearty game dishes and roast red meats.

STYLE
Rich & Full-bodied Red Wines

GRAPE VARIETY
Sangiovese, Canaiolo

BACKSTORY
The wonderful sloping hills of Tuscany are home to many great wines, but Chianti Classico is the oldest and most famous region, first delimited in 1739 when it supplied wine to the great noble families. Interpretations vary, but a Riserva, made only in the best vintages, should be a long-lived structured wine that represents the Sangiovese grape at its very best.

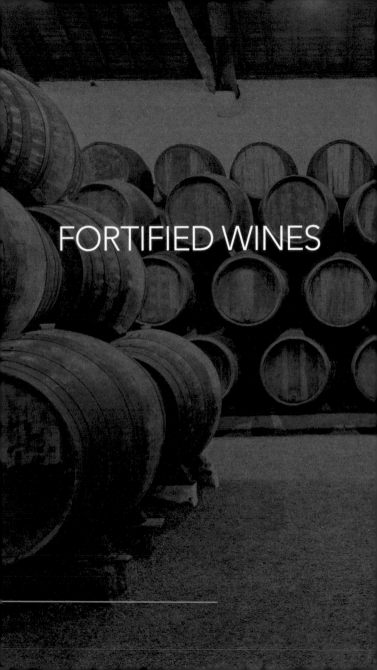

FORTIFIED WINES

119 La Iña Fino Sherry
Spain 15% €15.99

STOCKISTS: Mitchell & Son, IFSC, Sandycove and Avoca, Kilmacanogue; McCabes, Blackrock & Foxrock.

253

La Iña Fino Sherry

TASTING NOTE
Very appealing tangy fresh dry wine with nuts, green apples and a bracing salinity.

DRINK WITH
Serve well chilled with tapas; toasted almonds jamón iberico, olives, tortilla and cheeses.

STYLE
Fortified

GRAPE VARIETY
Palamino Fino

BACKSTORY
This book would not be complete without my favourite aperitif - a fino sherry. My idea of heaven is sitting in the shade on a sunny day in Jerez (or anywhere else for that matter), with a few slices of jamón iberico in front of me, alongside a chilled glass of fino.

120 Warre's Late Bottled Vintage Port 2003
Portugal 20% €35

255

STOCKISTS: Drinkstore, Stoneybatter; Donnybrook Fair; On the Grapevince, Dalkey; The Vintry, Rathgar; Village off-licence, Castleknock; Egan's, Portlaoise; Martin's, Fairview; Bradley's, Cork; The Wine Well, Dunboyne; O'Keefe's, Kilcock; O'Sullivan's, Tralee; The Wine Centre, Kilkenny; Rowan's, Rathfarnham.

Warre's Late Bottled Vintage Port 2003

TASTING NOTE
Rich plums with Christmas cake spice and dark chocolate. Sweet, but not too sweet, with a seductive long finish.

DRINK WITH
Blue cheese is traditional but any cheese will do fine. Hard cheeses work very well; so too does dark chocolate.

STYLE
Fortified

GRAPE VARIETY
Touriga Nacional, Tinto Barroca, Tinto Roriz, Touriga Franca

BACKSTORY
Warre's LBV is rated by most critics (including this one) and many consumers as the finest Late Bottled Vintage port on the market. Made in a traditional manner, it is bottled unfiltered, so stand it up for a day or two, or better still decant, before drinking.

121 Barbeito 10 Year Old Reserve Sercial Madeira
Portugal 19% **€37.99**

BARBEITO
MADEIRA

10
ANOS
YEARS OLD

SERCIAL
RESERVA VELHA
Vinho MADEIRA Wine

STOCKISTS: Wines on the Green; 64wine, Glasthule; Redmond's, Ranelagh.

Barbeito 10 Year Old Reserve Sercial Madeira

TASTING NOTE

Lifted piercing flavours of burnt orange skin, marmalade and toasted nuts, finishing bone dry. Complex and quite wonderful.

DRINK WITH

A stunning aperitif, served lightly chilled with a few nuts and other nibbles.

STYLE

Fortified

GRAPE VARIETY

Sercial

BACKSTORY

Madeira is one of the least-known fortified wines, but also one of the very best. From an island off the coast of Africa, this historic drink is heated for lengthy periods during production, making it almost indestructible. Once opened a bottle will keep for months without the aid of any gadgets. It comes in dry, medium and sweet styles, Sercial being the driest.

122

Fonseca Quinta do Panascal Vintage Port 2001
Portugal 20.5% **€44.95**

STOCKISTS: The Corkscrew @ Kenny's Lucan; The Corkscrew Chatham St. D2; Jus de Vine, Portmarnock; Deveney's, Dundrum.

Fonseca Quinta do Panascal Vintage Port 2001

TASTING NOTE
Rich, smooth, voluptuous, brooding, dark fruits with raisins and figs. Exceptional Port.

DRINK WITH
You could try a chocolate dessert, but the traditional-ist in me would seek out a plate of firm cheeses with a handful of walnuts.

STYLE
Fortified

GRAPE VARIETY
Touriga Nacional, Tinto Barroca, Tinto Roriz, Touriga Franca

BACKSTORY
Fonseca is one of the great old names in port. They have a reputation for producing wines with enticingly rich ripe sweet fruits. This is one of the finest examples I have tasted in years.

123 **Bodegas Tradición
Palo Cortado
VORS Sherry**
Spain 19.5% **€84.99**

STOCKISTS: Wines on the Green, Dawson St.; Black Pig, Donnbrook.

Bodegas Tradición Palo Cortado VORS Sherry

TASTING NOTE
Utterly amazing, elegant, complex nose with toasted almonds, furniture polish and old wood; sounds terrible but it is fantastic. You could sniff it all day or dab it behind your ears. The palate has more toasted almonds, a funky, earthy note, and a saline touch. Finishes bone dry and lasts for ever.

DRINK WITH
Best sipped with a plate of nuts (walnuts or toasted almonds would be good), and a hunk of firm cheese.

STYLE
Fortified

GRAPE VARIETY
Palamino Fino

BACKSTORY
A very expensive wine but a tasting last May of the wines of Bodegas Tradición was one of my highlights of the year. This is one of the very finest sherry houses, responsible for a range of exquisite old wines. Palo Cortado is a mystery sherry; nobody is quite sure how it is made - or makes itself in fact. It is best described as a Fino/Oloroso hybrid, with the intense grilled nut flavours of Oloroso combined with the freshness of a Fino. Sounds weird but they taste great, this one in particular. VORS on a sherry label means that the wine is a minimum of 30 years old

INDEX OF WINES

Domaine Eian da Ros Abouriou, Côtes du Marmandais 2012	**199**
Domaine Larue Puligny-Montrachet 1er cru La Garenne 2013	**115**
Doña Paula Estate Malbec 2014, Uco Valley	**229**
El Grano Chardonnay 2013, Poda Corta, Curico Valley (Organic)	**97**
F.X. Pichler Grüner Veltliner Loibner Loibenberg 2012, Wachau	**117**
Fonseca Quinta do Panascal Vintage Port 2001	**259**
FP Branco 2013, Filipa Pato, IGP Beira Atlantico, Portugal	**41**
Framingham Sauvignon Blanc 2014, Marlborough	**79**
Francesco Drusian Prosecco Colfondo NV	**7**
Frappato 2013, IGP Terre Siciliane	**123**
Frunza Pinot Noir 2014, Romania	**121**
Fürst Spätburgunder Tradition 2011, Franken	**157**
Gaia S 2010, Koutsi Hillside Vineyard, Peleponnisos, Greece	**237**
Grauburgunder 2013, Wagner Stempel, Rheinhessen	**111**
Greystone Pinot Noir 2012, Waipara	**159**
Greywacke Wild Sauvignon Blanc 2013, Marlborough	**89**
Hacienda Lopez de Haro Rioja Crianza 2011	**131**
Haute Côt(e) de Fruit 2104, Fabien Jouves, Cahors	**183**
Hirsch Kammern Renner Grüner Veltliner 2013, Kamptal	**51**
Hugel Cuvée des Amours 2012, Pinot Blanc de Blancs	**69**
Hunky Dory Sauvignon Blanc 2013, Marlborough	**43**
Il Molino di Grace 2012 Chianti Classico	**201**
J. Regnaudot Bourgogne Pinot Noir 2013	**143**
Jean Bousquet Cabernet Sauvignon 2013, Tupungato Valley	**225**
Ka Manciné Rossesse di Dolceacqua Bergana 2014	**155**
Kooyong Chardonnay 2012, Mornington Peninsula	**91**
La Ina Fino Sherry	**253**
La Maldicíon Tinto para beber de Marc Isart 2014 D.O. Madrid	**133**
La Malkerida 2012, Utiel-Requena	**187**
La Penetencia 2013 Ribera Sacra	**163**
La Rosca Cava Brut NV	**5**
Langhe Rosso 2013 Maretti	**141**
Larmandier Bernier Latitude Extra Brut NV	**13**
Le Grand Blanc, Comte Phillippe de Bertier 2012	**99**
Le Salare Montepulciano d'Abruzzo 2013	**137**
Le Vin d'Adrien 2014 Domaine de l'Amauve Côtes du Rhône	**227**
Les Auzines Cuvée Hautes Terres 2011 Corbières	**179**
Libido 2013 Navarra, David Sampedro Gil	**221**
Cimarosa Marlborough Sauvignon Blanc 2014	**55**
Lombeline Sauvignon Blanc 2014 Vin de Loire	**25**
Malat Grüner Veltliner Höhlgraben 2014, Kremstal	**47**
Marc Kreydenweiss Pinot Blanc Kritt 2014, Alsace	**103**
Mas de Daumas Gassac Blanc 2014	**93**
Menade Rueda V3 2013	**87**
Monte da Peceguina Red 2013, Herdade de Malhadinha Nova	**203**

INDEX OF STOCKISTS

STOCKISTS CONTINUED	Style	Price	Page No.
BAGGOT STREET WINES			
FP Branco 2013, Filipa Pato, Portugal	White	€ 18.70	41
Tramin Pinot Grigio 2014	White	€ 15.99	61
Cucu GV Verdejo 2013, El Barco del Corneta	White	€ 17.00	63
Celler Pardas Rupestris 2013, Penedes	White	€ 17.60	67
El Grano Chardonnay 2013, Poda Corta	White	€ 15.90	97
DMZ Chenin Blanc 2014, DeMorgenzon	White	€ 18.00	105
J. Regnaudot Bourgogne Pinot Noir 2013	Red	€ 18.25	143
Castro de Valtuille 2013 Bierzo	Red	€ 13.50	173
Pegos Claros 2010, Palmela	Red	€ 14.99	185
Monte da Peceguina 2013	Red	€ 20.95	203
Rafael Cambra El Bon Homme 2014	Red	€ 14.00	219
Ch. Musar 2007, Bekaa Valley, Lebanon	Red	€ 36.99	247
BALLYMALOE COOKERY SCHOOL GARDEN SHOP			
Menade Rueda V3 2013	White	€ 27.75	87
BEAN & BERRY, WEXFORD			
Custoza 2014 Cantina di Custoza, Veneto	White	€ 12.95	29
Ziereisen Tschuppen 2012, Badischer Landwein	Red	€ 24.00	153
BLACK PIG, DONNYBROOK			
FP Branco 2013, Filipa Pato, Portugal	White	€ 18.70	41
Cucu GV Verdejo 2013, El Barco del Corneta	White	€ 17.00	63
Castro de Valtuille 2013 Bierzo	Red	€ 13.50	173
Artuke Pies Negros 2013 Rioja	Red	€ 18.90	197
Dom Rafael 2012, Mouchâo, Alentejo	Red	€ 14.50	223
Bodegas Tradición Palo Cortado VORS	Fortified	€ 84.99	261
BLACKROCK CELLAR			
Custoza 2014 Cantina di Custoza, Veneto	White	€ 12.95	29
FP Branco 2013, Filipa Pato, Portugal	White	€ 18.70	41
Hunky Dory Sauvignon Blanc 2013, Marlborough	White	€ 18.99	43
Tramin Pinot Grigio 2014	White	€ 15.99	61
Greywacke Wild Sauvignon Blanc 2013,	White	€ 33.00	89
El Grano Chardonnay 2013, Poda Corta	White	€ 15.90	97
DMZ Chenin Blanc 2014, DeMorgenzon	White	€ 18.00	105
J. Regnaudot Bourgogne Pinot Noir 2013	Red	€ 18.25	143
Castro de Valtuille 2013 Bierzo	Red	€ 13.50	173
Oveja Tinta 2014, Bodegas Fontana	Red	€ 13.99	177
Valli Unite 'Ottavio Ruben Rosso' 2013	Red	€ 14.55	181
Rafael Cambra El Bon Homme 2014	Red	€ 14.00	219
Bodega Colomé Estate 2012, Cafayate	Red	€ 24.99	241
Ridge East Bench Zinfandel 2013, California	Red	€ 29.95	245

	Style	Price	Page No.
STOCKISTS CONTINUED			

BRADLEY'S CORK
Wiston Estate Blanc de Blancs NV	Sparkling	€ 53.00	11
Nyetimber Classic Cuvée 2010	Sparkling	€ 59.99	15
Jean Bousquet Cabernet Sauvignon 2013	Red	€ 15.50	225
Ch. Musar 2007, Bekaa Valley, Lebanon	Red	€ 36.99	247
Warre's Bottle-aged Late Bottled Port 2003	Fortified	€ 35.00	255

CABOT & CO, WESTPORT
Nyetimber Classic Cuvée 2010	Sparkling	€ 59.99	15
Wittmann Riesling 2014, Rheinhessen	White	€ 22.00	45
Roka Blaufränkisch 2013, Stajerska	Red	€ 15.99	139
Moric Blaufränkisch 2012, Burgenland	Red	€ 22.99	149
Fürst Spätburgunder Tradition 2011, Franken	Red	€ 30.00	157

CAFÉ RUA, CASTLEBAR
Lombeline Sauvignon Blanc 2014 Vin de Loire	White	€ 11.00	25
Castello di Verduna Barbera d'Alba 2013	Red	€ 21.50	147

CARPENTER'S, CASTLEKNOCK
Hunky Dory Sauvignon Blanc 2013, Marlborough	White	€ 18.99	43

THE CHEESE PANTRY, DUBLIN 8
Anima Umbra 2012, Arnaldo Caprai, Umbria	Red	€ 14.50	129

CLONTARF WINES
Tramin Pinot Grigio 2014	White	€ 15.99	61
Cucu GV Verdejo 2013, El Barco del Corneta	White	€ 17.00	63
Celler Pardas Rupestris 2013, Penedes	White	€ 17.60	67
Hugel Cuvée des Amours 2012, Pinot Blanc	White	€ 17.99	69
Greywacke Wild Sauvignon Blanc 2013,	White	€ 33.00	89
Anima Umbra 2012, Arnaldo Caprai, Umbria	Red	€ 14.50	129
Greystone Pinot Noir 2012, Waipara	Red	€ 34.00	159
La Penetencia 2013 Ribera Sacra	Red	€ 50.00	163
Castro de Valtuille 2013 Bierzo	Red	€ 13.50	173
Artuke Pies Negros 2013 Rioja	Red	€ 18.90	197
Dom Rafael 2012, Mouchâo, Alentejo	Red	€ 14.50	223
Bodega Colomé Estate 2012, Cafayate	Red	€ 24.99	241

THE COUNTER, LETTERKENNY
Dog Point Vineyard Sauvignon Blanc 2014	White	€ 23.95	85
Ridge East Bench Zinfandel 2013, California	Red	€ 29.95	245

STOCKISTS CONTINUED	Style	Price	Page No.
THE CORKSCREW, CHATHAM STREET			
Wiston Estate Blanc de Blancs NV	Sparkling	€ 53.00	11
Nyetimber Classic Cuvée 2010	Sparkling	€ 59.99	15
Champagne Deutz Rosé NV Champagne	Sparkling	€ 65.00	19
Custoza 2014 Cantina di Custoza, Veneto	White	€ 12.95	29
Wieninger Wiener Gemischter Satz 2014	White	€ 17.95	39
Hirsch Grüner Veltliner 2013, Kamptal	White	€ 34.95	51
Dog Point Vineyard Sauvignon Blanc 2014	White	€ 23.95	85
Menade Rueda V3 2013	White	€ 27.75	87
Greywacke Wild Sauvignon Blanc 2013	White	€ 33.00	89
DMZ Chenin Blanc 2014, DeMorgenzon	White	€ 18.00	105
Antão Vaz da Peceguina 2014	White	€ 19.95	109
Grauburgunder 2013, Wagner Stempel	White	€ 19.95	111
d'Arenberg Lucky Lizard Chardonnay 2012	White	€ 22.00	113
J. Regnaudot Bourgogne Pinot Noir 2013	Red	€ 18.25	143
Muhr Van der Niepoort Samt & Seide 2012	Red	€ 23.00	151
Ka Manciné Rossesse di Dolceacqua 2014	Red	€ 26.00	155
Bodega Colomé Estate 2012, Cafayate	Red	€ 24.99	241
Ch. Musar 2007, Bekaa Valley, Lebanon	Red	€ 36.99	247
Casa Emma Chianti Classico Riserva 2010	Red	€ 39.95	249
Fonseca Q. do Panascal Vintage Port 2001	Fortified	€ 44.95	259
THE CORKSCREW@KENNY'S, LUCAN			
Wieninger Wiener Gemischter Satz 2014	White	€ 17.95	39
Hirsch Grüner Veltliner 2013, Kamptal	White	€ 34.95	51
Casa Emma Chianti Classico Riserva 2010	Red	€ 39.95	249
Fonseca Q. do Panascal Vintage Port 2001	Fortified	€ 44.95	259
CURIOUS WINES, CORK & NAAS			
Mas de Daumas Gassac Blanc 2014	White	€ 45.00	93
D6, HAROLD'S CROSS DUBLIN 6			
Greystone Pinot Noir 2012, Waipara	Red	€ 34.00	159
DALY'S, BOYLE, CO. ROSCOMMON			
Jean Bousquet Cabernet Sauvignon 2013	Red	€ 15.50	225
DEVENEY'S, DUNDRUM			
Domaine de Pellehaut, Gascogne 2014	White	€ 12.99	57
DMZ Chenin Blanc 2014, DeMorgenzon	White	€ 18.00	105
Greystone Pinot Noir 2012, Waipara	Red	€ 34.00	159
Monte da Peceguina Red 2013,	Red	€ 20.95	203
Bodega Colomé Estate 2012, Cafayate	Red	€ 24.99	241

DEVENEY'S, RATHMINES

Terre d'Eglantier Réserve, Ardechois 2013	White	€ 16.95	101
Pegos Claros 2010, Palmela	Red	€ 14.99	185
Monte da Peceguina Red 2013	Red	€ 20.95	203

DICEY RILEY'S, BALLYSHANNON

Dog Point Vineyard Sauvignon Blanc 2014	White	€ 23.95	85

DONNYBROOK FAIR

Nyetimber Classic Cuvée 2010	Sparkling	€ 59.99	15
Blanc d'Ogier 2012, M&S Ogier	White	€ 22.75	81
Greywacke Wild Sauvignon Blanc 2013	White	€ 33.00	89
Antão Vaz da Peceguina 2014	White	€ 19.95	109
Grauburgunder 2013, Wagner Stempel	White	€ 19.95	111
d'Arenberg Lucky Lizard Chardonnay 2012	White	€ 22.00	113
J. Regnaudot Bourgogne Pinot Noir 2013	Red	€ 18.25	143
Bourgogne Pinot Noir 2013, Patrice Cacheux	Red	€ 19.50	145
Muhr Van der Niepoort Samt & Seide 2012	Red	€ 23.00	151
Greystone Pinot Noir 2012, Waipara	Red	€ 34.00	159
Pegos Claros 2010, Palmela	Red	€ 14.99	185
Côtes du Rhône Les Deux Cols 2014	Red	€ 16.95	191
Monte da Peceguina Red 2013	Red	€ 20.95	203
Jean Bousquet Cabernet Sauvignon 2013	Red	€ 15.50	225
Bodega Colomé Estate 2012, Cafayate	Red	€ 24.99	241
Warre's Bottle-aged LBV Port 2003	Fortified	€ 35.00	255

DRINK STORE, DUBLIN 7

Cucu GV Verdejo 2013 El Barco del Corneta	White	€ 17.00	63
Blanc d'Ogier 2012, M&S Ogier	White	€ 22.75	81
DMZ Chenin Blanc 2014, DeMorgenzon	White	€ 18.00	105
Oveja Tinta 2014, Bodegas Fontana	Red	€ 13.99	177
Pegos Claros 2010, Palmela	Red	€ 14.99	185
Pascual Toso Malbec 2013, Mendoza	White	€ 13.99	217

DUNNES STORES

Carmen Right Wave Pinot Noir 2014	Red	€ 14.99	135
Aranleón Blés Tinto 2014, Valencia	Red	€ 11.00	169

EGAN'S, PORTLAOISE

d'Arenberg Lucky Lizard Chardonnay 2012	White	€ 22.00	113
Pascual Toso Malbec 2013, Mendoza	White	€ 13.99	217

STOCKISTS CONTINUED	Style	Price	Page No.
ENNIS BUTCHERS, SOUTH CIRCULAR ROAD			
Cucu GV Verdejo 2013, El Barco del Corneta	White	€ 17.00	63
Anima Umbra 2012, Arnaldo Caprai, Umbria	Red	€ 14.50	129
Artuke Pies Negros 2013 Rioja	Red	€ 18.90	197
FALLON & BYRNE, EXCHEQUER STREET			
Nyetimber Classic Cuvée 2010	Sparkling	€ 59.99	15
Framingham Sauvignon Blanc 2014	White	€ 19.75	79
J. Regnaudot Bourgogne Pinot Noir 2013	Red	€ 18.25	143
Castro de Valtuille 2013 Bierzo	Red	€ 13.50	173
Valli Unite 'Ottavio Ruben Rosso' 2013	Red	€ 14.55	181
Pegos Claros 2010, Palmela	Red	€ 14.99	185
Monte da Peceguina Red 2013	Red	€ 20.95	203
Villa di Capezzana Carmignano 2011	Red	€ 34.99	207
Rafael Cambra El Bon Homme 2014	Red	€ 14.00	219
Bodega Colomé Estate 2012, Cafayate	Red	€ 24.99	241
FINE WINES, NATIONWIDE			
Greywacke Wild Sauvignon Blanc 2013	White	€ 33.00	89
FRESH OUTLETS			
Tramin Pinot Grigio 2014	White	€ 15.99	61
Antão Vaz da Peceguina 2014	White	€ 19.95	109
Frunza Pinot Noir 2014, Romania	Red	€ 9.99	121
Monte da Peceguina Red 2013	Red	€ 20.95	203
GIBNEY'S, MALAHIDE			
Tramin Pinot Grigio 2014	White	€ 15.99	61
Frunza Pinot Noir 2014, Romania	Red	€ 9.99	121
Greystone Pinot Noir 2012, Waipara	Red	€ 34.00	159
GREENACRES, WEXFORD			
Bründlmayer Kamptaler Riesling 2013	White	€ 17.50	65
Carmen Gran Reserva Chardonnay 2013	White	€ 18.50	107
Muhr Van der Niepoort Samt & Seide 2012	Red	€ 23.00	151
GREEN MAN WINES, TERENURE			
Wiston Estate Blanc de Blancs NV	Sparkling	€ 53.00	11
Nyetimber Classic Cuvée 2010	Sparkling	€ 59.99	15
FP Branco 2013, Filipa Pato, Portugal	White	€ 18.70	41
Cucu GV Verdejo 2013, El Barco del Corneta	White	€ 17.00	63
Celler Pardas Rupestris 2013, Penedes	White	€ 17.60	67
Framingham Sauvignon Blanc 2014	White	€ 19.75	79
Greywacke Wild Sauvignon Blanc 2013	White	€ 33.00	89
El Grano Chardonnay 2013, Poda Corta	White	€ 15.90	97

STOCKISTS CONTINUED	Style	Price	Page No.
Dom. Larue Puligny-Montrachet 1er cru 2013	White	€ 49.50	115
Hacienda Lopez de Haro Rioja Crianza 2011	Red	€ 14.50	131
Langhe Rosso 2013 Maretti	Red	€ 17.90	141
J. Regnaudot Bourgogne Pinot Noir 2013	Red	€ 18.25	143
La Penetencia 2013 Ribera Sacra	Red	€ 50.00	163
Ata Rangi Pinot Noir 2013, Martinborough	Red	€ 63.99	165
Valli Unite 'Ottavio Ruben Rosso' 2013	Red	€ 14.55	181
La Malkerida 2012, Utiel-Requena	Red	€ 15.95	187
7, rue de Pompe 2013, Mas Coutelou	Red	€ 16.50	189
Monte da Peceguina Red 2013	Red	€ 20.95	203
Villa di Capezzana Carmignano 2011	Red	€ 34.99	207
TolpuddleVineyard Pinot Noir 2013	Red	€ 59.99	211
Rafael Cambra El Bon Homme 2014	Red	€ 14.00	219
Quellu' Cinsault 2013 Louis-Antoine Luyt	Red	€ 23.90	239
Bodega Colomé Estate 2012, Cafayate	Red	€ 24.99	241

HARGADON'S, SLIGO

Dog Point Vineyard Sauvignon Blanc 2014	White	€ 23.95	85

THE HOLE IN THE WALL DUBLIN 7

Champagne Vilmart Grand Cellier Brut	Sparkling	€ 62.00	17
Custoza 2014 Cantina di Custoza, Veneto	White	€ 12.95	29
Terre d'Eglantier Réserve, V. Ardechois 2013	White	€ 16.95	101
Dom Rafael 2012, Mouchâo, Alentejo	Red	€ 14.50	223

JNWINE.COM

Sartarelli Verdicchio dei Castelli di Jesi 2014	White	€ 14.99	31
Sancerre Florès 2013 Vincent Pinard	White	€ 29.50	49
Soalheiro Alvarinho 2014 Vinho Verde	White	€ 18.99	75
Dog Point Vineyard Sauvignon Blanc 2014	White	€ 23.95	85
Ridge East Bench Zinfandel 2013, California	Red	€ 29.95	245

JOHN R'S, LISTOWEL

Le Salare Montepulciano d'Abruzzo 2013	Red	€ 14.99	137

JUS DE VINE, PORTMARNOCK

Nyetimber Classic Cuvée 2010	Sparkling	€ 59.99	15
Champagne Deutz Rosé NV Champagne	Sparkling	€ 65.00	19
Veuve Cliquot Ponsardin Rosé 2004	Sparkling	€ 80.00	21
Lombeline Sauvignon Blanc 2014, Loire	White	€ 11.00	25
Muscadet, Clos des Montys 2014	White	€ 15.50	35
Tramin Pinot Grigio 2014	White	€ 15.99	61
Hugel Cuvée des Amours 2012, Pinot Blanc	White	€ 17.99	69
Greywacke Wild Sauvignon Blanc 2013	White	€ 33.00	89

STOCKISTS CONTINUED	Style	Price	Page No.
Hacienda Lopez de Haro Rioja Crianza 2011	Red	€ 14.50	131
Langhe Rosso 2013 Maretti	Red	€ 17.90	141
Nuits St. Georges, 2010 Maison Ambroise	Red	€ 46.35	161
Pegos Claros 2010, Palmela	Red	€ 14.99	185
7, rue de Pompe 2013, Mas Coutelou	Red	€ 16.50	189
Côtes du Rhône Les Deux Cols, 2014	Red	€ 16.95	191
Villa di Capezzana Carmignano 2011	Red	€ 34.99	207
TolpuddleVineyard Pinot Noir 2013	Red	€ 59.99	211
Pascual Toso Malbec 2013, Mendoza	White	€ 13.99	217
Dom Rafael 2012, Mouchâo, Alentejo	Red	€ 14.50	223
Ribeo 2011, Morellino di Scansano	Red	€ 18.99	233
Bodega Colomé Estate 2012, Cafayate	Red	€ 24.99	241

KINNEGAR.COM

Sijnn Red 2010	Red	€ 25.00	243

LE CAVEAU, KILKENNY

Wiston Estate Blanc de Blancs NV	Sparkling	€ 53.00	11
Birgit Eichinger Grüner Veltliner, 2014	White	€ 19.00	77
Framingham Sauvignon Blanc 2014	White	€ 19.75	79
Menade Rueda V3 2013	White	€ 27.75	87
El Grano Chardonnay 2013, Poda Corta	White	€ 15.90	97
Dom. Larue Puligny-Montrachet 1er cru 2013	White	€ 49.50	115
J. Regnaudot Bourgogne Pinot Noir 2013	Red	€ 18.25	143
Nuits St. Georges 2010 Maison Ambroise	Red	€ 46.35	161
Valli Unite 'Ottavio Ruben Rosso' 2013	Red	€ 14.55	181
Quellu' Cinsault 2013 Louis-Antoine Luyt	Red	€ 23.90	239

LIDL

Cimarosa Marlborough Sauvignon Blanc 2014	White	€ 8.79	55

LISTON'S, CAMDEN STREET

Lombeline Sauvignon Blanc 2014 Loire	White	€ 11.00	25
Custoza 2014 Cantina di Custoza	White	€ 12.95	29
Anima Umbra 2012, Arnaldo Caprai	Red	€ 14.50	129
J. Regnaudot Bourgogne Pinot Noir 2013	Red	€ 18.25	143
Pegos Claros 2010, Palmela	Red	€ 14.99	185
Monte da Peceguina Red 2013	Red	€ 20.95	203

THE LOOP, DUBLIN AIRPORT

Santa Rita Casa Real 2011, Maipo Valley	Red	€ 49.95	209

STOCKISTS CONTINUED	Style	Price	Page No.

MANNING'S EMPORIUM, BALLICKEY, CO. CORK

Greywacke Wild Sauvignon Blanc 2013	White	€ 33.00	89

MARKS & SPENCER

Zibibbo 2013, Terre Siciliane	White	€ 12.29	27
Frappato 2013, IGP Terre Siciliane	Red	€ 12.29	123
Perricone Caruso e Minini 2013 Sicilia	Red	€ 12.29	171

MARTIN'S OFF-LICENCE, FAIRVIEW

Tramin Pinot Grigio 2014, Alto-Adige Sud-Tirol	White	€ 15.99	61
Greywacke Wild Sauvignon Blanc 2013	White	€ 33.00	89
d'Arenberg Lucky Lizard Chardonnay 2012	White	€ 22.00	113
Oveja Tinta 2014, Bodegas Fontana	Red	€ 13.99	177
Dom Rafael 2012, Mouchâo, Alentejo	Red	€ 14.50	223

MCCABE'S, BLACKROCK & FOXROCK

Lombeline Sauvignon Blanc 2014 Loire	White	€ 11.00	25
Tramin Pinot Grigio 2014	White	€ 15.99	61
Bourgogne Pinot Noir 2013, Patrice Cacheux	Red	€ 19.50	145
Pascual Toso Malbec 2013, Mendoza	White	€ 13.99	217
Ribeo 2011, Morellino di Scansano	Red	€ 18.99	233
La Ina Fino Sherry	Fortified	€ 15.99	253

MCCAMBRIDGES, GALWAY

Roka Blaufränkisch 2013, Stajerska	Red	€ 15.99	139
Moric Blaufränkisch 2012, Burgenland	Red	€ 22.99	149

MCFADDEN'S, LETTERKENNY

Wieninger Wiener Gemischter Satz 2014	White	€ 17.95	39

MICHAEL'S WINES, DEERPARK

Francesco Drusian Prosecco Colfondo NV	Sparkling	€ 17.95	7
Custoza 2014 Cantina di Custoza, Veneto	White	€ 12.95	29
Celler Pardas Rupestris 2013, Penedes	White	€ 17.60	67
La Malkerida 2012, Utiel-Requena	Red	€ 15.95	187
Villa di Capezzana Carmignano 2011	Red	€ 34.99	207

MITCHELL & SON, IFSC, SANDYCOVE AND AVOCA, KILMACANOGUE

Nyetimber Classic Cuvée 2010	Sparkling	€ 59.99	15
Domaine de Pellehaut Gascogne 2014	White	€ 12.99	57
Birgit Eichinger Grüner Veltliner 2014	White	€ 19.00	77
Menade Rueda V3 2013	White	€ 27.75	87

STOCKISTS CONTINUED	Style	Price	Page No.
Greywacke Wild Sauvignon Blanc 2013	White	€ 33.00	89
Castello di Verduna Barbera d'Alba 2013	Red	€ 21.50	147
Pegos Claros 2010, Palmela	Red	€ 14.99	185
Monte da Peceguina Red 2013	Red	€ 20.95	203
Celler Lafou El Sender 2013 Terra Alta	Red	€ 19.95	235
Bodega Colomé Estate 2012, Cafayate	Red	€ 24.99	241
Sijnn Red 2010	Red	€ 25.00	243
Ch. Musar 2007, Bekaa Valley, Lebanon	Red	€ 36.99	247
La Ina Fino Sherry	Red	€ 15.99	253

MOLLOY'S LIQUOR STORES, DUBLIN

Le Grand Blanc, Comte Phillippe de Bertier 2012	White	€ 15.95	99
Ch. Musar 2007, Bekaa Valley, Lebanon	Red	€ 36.99	247

MORTON'S, GALWAY

Wittmann Riesling 2014, Rheinhessen	White	€ 22.00	45
Moric Blaufränkisch 2012, Burgenland	Red	€ 22.99	149
Muhr Van der Niepoort Samt & Seide 2012	Red	€ 23.00	151

MORTON'S, RANELAGH

Custoza 2014 Cantina di Custoza	White	€ 12.95	29
DMZ Chenin Blanc 2014, DeMorgenzon	White	€ 18.00	105
Frunza Pinot Noir 2014, Romania	Red	€ 9.99	121
Pegos Claros 2010, Palmela	Red	€ 14.99	185
Monte da Peceguina Red 2013	Red	€ 20.95	203

MYLES DOYLE, GOREY

Domaine de Pellehaut, Gascogne 2014	White	€ 12.99	57

NECTAR WINES, SANDYFORD

Custoza 2014 Cantina di Custoza, Veneto	White	€ 12.95	29
Pegos Claros 2010, Palmela	Red	€ 14.99	185
Monte da Peceguina Red 2013	Red	€ 20.95	203

NOLAN'S, CLONTARF

Tramin Pinot Grigio 2014	White	€ 15.99	61
Pascual Toso Malbec 2013, Mendoza	White	€ 13.99	217
Jean Bousquet Cabernet Sauvignon 2013	Red	€ 15.50	225

NO.1 PERY SQUARE, LIMERICK

Muscadet, Clos des Montys 2014	White	€ 15.50	35

STOCKISTS CONTINUED	Style	Price	Page No.
Wittmann Riesling 2014, Rheinhessen	White	€ 22.00	45
Roka Blaufränkisch 2013, Stajerska	Red	€ 15.99	139
Moric Blaufränkisch 2012, Burgenland	Red	€ 22.99	149
Fürst Spätburgunder Tradition 2011	Red	€ 30.00	157
Côtes du Rhône Les Deux Cols, 2014	Red	€ 16.95	191

NO. 21 MIDLETON, CO. CORK
Hunky Dory Sauvignon Blanc 2013	White	€ 18.99	43

O'BRIENS
La Rosca Cava Brut NV	Sparkling	€ 14.99	5
Beaumont de Crayeres NV Champagne	Sparkling	€ 36.99	9
Veuve Cliquot Ponsardin Rosé 2004	Sparkling	€ 80.00	21
Sauvignon Blanc Les Hautes Lieux 2014	White	€ 15.49	33
Domaine de Begude 11300 Chardonnay	White	€ 17.99	71
Pazo de Señorans 2013, Rías Baixas	White	€ 22.99	83
Marc Kreydenweiss Pinot Blanc Kritt 2014	White	€ 17.99	103
Caves Saint-Désirat Syrah 2013 Ardèche	Red	€ 14.49	127
Ata Rangi Pinot Noir 2013, Martinborough	Red	€ 63.99	165
Aranleón Encuentro 2014, DOP Valencia	Red	€ 13.99	175
Les Auzines Cuvée H. Terres 2011 Corbières	Red	€ 14.49	179
Pegos Claros 2010, Palmela	Red	€ 14.99	185
Astrolabe Pinot Noir 2010	Red	€ 25.49	205
Porta 6 2011 Lisboa	Red	€ 12.99	215
Doña Paula Estate Malbec 2014	Red	€ 15.99	229
Gaia S 2010, Koutsi Hillside Vineyard	Red	€ 23.49	237
Ch. Musar 2007, Bekaa Valley, Lebanon	Red	€ 36.99	247

O'DONOVAN'S, CORK
Pegos Claros 2010, Palmela	Red	€ 14.99	185
Monte da Peceguina Red 2013	Red	€ 20.95	203

O'DRISCOLL'S, CAHIRCIVEEN
Hunky Dory Sauvignon Blanc 2013	White	€ 18.99	43

O'DRISCOLL'S, BALLINLOUGH
Ch. Musar 2007, Bekaa Valley, Lebanon	Red	€ 36.99	247

O'LEARY'S, COOTEHILL, CO. CAVAN
La Malkerida 2012, Utiel-Requena	Red	€ 15.95	187

ON THE GRAPEVINE, DALKEY

Wieninger Wiener Gemischter Satz 2014	White	€ 17.95	39
Wittmann Riesling 2014, Rheinhessen	White	€ 22.00	45
Roka Blaufränkisch 2013, Stajerska	Red	€ 15.99	139
J. Regnaudot Bourgogne Pinot Noir 2013	Red	€ 18.25	143
Moric Blaufränkisch 2012, Burgenland	Red	€ 22.99	149
Fürst Spätburgunder Tradition 2011	Red	€ 30.00	157
Ata Rangi Pinot Noir 2013, Martinborough	Red	€ 63.99	165
Pegos Claros 2010, Palmela	Red	€ 14.99	185
Monte da Peceguina Red 2013	Red	€ 20.95	203
Dom Rafael 2012, Mouchão, Alentejo	Red	€ 14.50	223
Casa Emma Chianti Classico Riserva 2010	Red	€ 39.95	249

THE PARTING GLASS, ENNISKERRY

d'Arenberg Lucky Lizard Chardonnay 2012	White	€ 22.00	113

POWER & SMULLEN, LUCAN

Dog Point Vineyard Sauvignon Blanc 2014	White	€ 23.95	85
Greystone Pinot Noir 2012, Waipara	Red	€ 34.00	159
Pegos Claros 2010, Palmela	Red	€ 14.99	185
La Malkerida 2012, Utiel-Requena	Red	€ 15.95	187
Monte da Peceguina Red 2013	Red	€ 20.95	203

PROBUS WINES, FENIAN STREET

Domaine de Pellehaut, Gascogne 2014	White	€ 12.99	57
DMZ Chenin Blanc 2014, DeMorgenzon	White	€ 18.00	105
Oveja Tinta 2014, Bodegas Fontana	Red	€ 13.99	177
Dom Rafael 2012, Mouchão, Alentejo	Red	€ 14.50	223

QUINTESSENTIAL WINES, DROGHEDA

Francesco Drusian Prosecco Colfondo NV	Sparkling	€ 17.95	7
Champagne Vilmart Grand Cellier Brut	Sparkling	€ 62.00	17
La Malkerida 2012, Utiel-Requena	Red	€ 15.95	187
Libido 2013 Navarra, David Sampedro Gil	Red	€ 14.50	221

RED ISLAND WINE, SKERRIES

Terre d'Eglantier Réserve, Ardechois 2013	White	€ 16.95	101
DMZ Chenin Blanc 2014, DeMorgenzon	White	€ 18.00	105
Castro de Valtuille 2013 Bierzo	Red	€ 13.50	173
Oveja Tinta 2014, Bodegas Fontana	Red	€ 13.99	177
Pegos Claros 2010, Palmela	Red	€ 14.99	185

STOCKISTS CONTINUED	Style	Price	Page No.
Monte da Peceguina Red 2013	Red	€ 20.95	203
Villa di Capezzana Carmignano 2011	Red	€ 34.99	207
Rafael Cambra El Bon Homme 2014	Red	€ 14.00	219

REDMOND'S, RANELAGH

	Style	Price	Page No.
Veuve Cliquot Ponsardin Rosé 2004	Sparkling	€ 80.00	21
Muscadet, Clos des Montys 2014	White	€ 15.50	35
Hugel Cuvée des Amours 2012, Pinot Blanc	White	€ 17.99	69
Birgit Eichinger Grüner Veltliner 2014	White	€ 19.00	77
Greywacke Wild Sauvignon Blanc 2013	White	€ 33.00	89
F.X. Pichler Grüner Veltliner Loibenberg 2012	White	€ 50.00	117
Anima Umbra 2012, Arnaldo Caprai, Umbria	Red	€ 14.50	129
J. Regnaudot Bourgogne Pinot Noir 2013	Red	€ 18.25	143
Muhr Van der Niepoort Samt & Seide 2012	Red	€ 23.00	151
Ziereisen Tschuppen 2012, Badischer Landwein	Red	€ 24.00	153
Greystone Pinot Noir 2012, Waipara	Red	€ 34.00	159
Pegos Claros 2010, Palmela	Red	€ 14.99	185
Artuke Pies Negros 2013 Rioja	Red	€ 18.90	197
Monte da Peceguina Red 2013	Red	€ 20.95	203
Villa di Capezzana Carmignano 2011	Red	€ 34.99	207
Santa Rita Casa Real 2011, Maipo Valley	Red	€ 49.95	209
TolpuddleVineyard Pinot Noir 2013	Red	€ 59.99	211
Rafael Cambra El Bon Homme 2014	Red	€ 14.00	219
Dom Rafael 2012, Mouchâo, Alentejo	Red	€ 14.50	223
Bodega Colomé Estate 2012, Cafayate	Red	€ 24.99	241
Barbeito 10 Year Old Reserve Sercial Madeira	Fortified	€ 37.99	257

RED NOSE WINES, CLONMEL

	Style	Price	Page No.
Mas de Daumas Gassac Blanc 2014	White	€ 45.00	93

SEARSONS, MONKSTOWN

	Style	Price	Page No.
Nyetimber Classic Cuvée 2010	Sparkling	€ 59.99	15
Malat Grüner Veltliner Höhlgraben 2014	White	€ 23.95	47
Villa di Capezzana Carmignano 2011	Red	€ 34.99	207
Dom Rafael 2012, Mouchâo, Alentejo	Red	€ 14.50	223
Côtes du Rhône 2013, Dom. Saint Gayan	Red	€ 16.95	231

SHERIDAN'S CHEESEMONGERS, GALWAY, DUBLIN & CARNAROSS, CO. MEATH

	Style	Price	Page No.
Sangoiovese Rubicone Medici Ermete	Red	€ 12.95	125
Le Salare Montepulciano d'Abruzzo 2013	Red	€ 14.99	137

STOCKISTS CONTINUED	Style	Price	Page No.
Castello di Verduna Barbera d'Alba 2013	Red	€ 21.50	147
SHIEL'S, MALAHIDE			
Hugel Cuvée des Amours 2012	White	€ 17.99	69
SUPERVALU			
Carmen Gran Reserva Chardonnay 2013	White	€ 18.50	107
Carmen Right Wave Pinot Noir 2014	Red	€ 14.99	135
Doña Paula Estate Malbec 2014, Uco Valley	Red	€ 15.99	229
Ch. Musar 2007, Bekaa Valley, Lebanon	Red	€ 36.99	247
SUPERVALU, SUTTON			
Custoza 2014 Cantina di Custoza, Veneto	White	€ 12.95	29
SWEENEY'S, HART'S CORNER, GLASNEVIN			
Carmen Gran Reserva Chardonnay 2013	White	€ 18.50	107
d'Arenberg Lucky Lizard Chardonnay 2012	White	€ 22.00	113
Castro de Valtuille 2013 Bierzo	Red	€ 13.50	173
Pegos Claros 2010, Palmela	Red	€ 14.99	185
Monte da Peceguina Red 2013	Red	€ 20.95	203
TERROIRS, DONNYBROOK Terroirs.ie			
Larmandier Bernier Latitude Extra Brut NV	Sparkling	€ 59.50	13
Sancerre Florès 2013 Vincent Pinard	White	€ 29.50	49
Ziereisen Tschuppen 2012, Badischer Landwein	Red	€ 24.00	153
Haute Côt(e) de Fruit 2104, Jouves, Cahors	Red	€ 14.95	183
Dom. Eian da Ros Abouriou, Marmandais 2012	Red	€ 19.50	199
TESCO			
Carmen Right Wave Pinot Noir 2014	Red	€ 14.99	135
Doña Paula Estate Malbec 2014, Uco Valley	Red	€ 15.99	229
THOMAS, FOXROCK			
Nyetimber Classic Cuvée 2010	Sparkling	€ 59.99	15
THOMAS WOODBERRY, GLAWAY			
Nyetimber Classic Cuvée 2010	Sparkling	€ 59.99	15
Wieninger Wiener Gemischter Satz 2014	White	€ 17.95	39
Greystone Pinot Noir 2012, Waipara	Red	€ 34.00	159
Bodega Colomé Estate 2012, Cafayate	Red	€ 24.99	241
Casa Emma Chianti Classico Riserva 2010	Red	€ 39.95	249

STOCKISTS CONTINUED	Style	Price	Page No.
THYME OUT, DALKEY			
Domaine de Pellehaut, Gascogne 2014	White	€ 12.99	57
LA TOUCHE WINE 4U, GREYSTONES			
Champagne Deutz Rosé NV Champagne	Sparkling	€ 65.00	19
Lombeline Sauvignon Blanc 2014, Loire	White	€ 11.00	25
Hunky Dory Sauvignon Blanc 2013	White	€ 18.99	43
Celler Pardas Rupestris 2013, Penedes	White	€ 17.60	67
Greywacke Wild Sauvignon Blanc 2013	White	€ 33.00	89
Antão Vaz da Peceguina 2014	White	€ 19.95	109
Le Salare Montepulciano d'Abruzzo 2013	Red	€ 14.99	137
Bourgogne Pinot Noir 2013, Patrice Cacheux	Red	€ 19.50	145
Muhr Van der Niepoort Samt & Seide 2012	Red	€ 23.00	151
Ziereisen Tschuppen 2012, Badischer Landwein	Red	€ 24.00	153
Greystone Pinot Noir 2012, Waipara	Red	€ 34.00	159
Pegos Claros 2010, Palmela	Red	€ 14.99	185
Monte da Peceguina Red 2013	Red	€ 20.95	203
THE VILLAGE, CASTLEKNOCK			
Champagne Deutz Rosé NV Champagne	Sparkling	€ 65.00	19
Warre's Bottle-aged Late Bottled Port 2003	Fortified	€ 35.00	255
THE VINTRY, RATHGAR ROAD, DUBLIN 6			
Tramin Pinot Grigio 2014, Alto-Adige Sud-Tirol	White	€ 15.99	61
Hugel Cuvée des Amours 2012, Pinot Blanc	White	€ 17.99	69
Carmen Gran Reserva Chardonnay 2013	White	€ 18.50	107
Frunza Pinot Noir 2014, Romania	Red	€ 9.99	121
WHELEHAN'S WINES, LOUGHLINSTOWN			
La Grange 2013 Dom. Luneau-Papin Muscadet	White	€ 15.95	37
Dog Point Vineyard Sauvignon Blanc 2014	White	€ 23.95	85
Kooyong Chardonnay 2012, Mornington	White	€ 33.95	91
Castro de Valtuille 2013 Bierzo	Red	€ 13.50	173
Pegos Claros 2010, Palmela	Red	€ 14.99	185
Il Molino di Grace 2012 Chianti Classico	Red	€ 19.95	201
Monte da Peceguina Red 2013	Red	€ 20.95	203
Dom. de l'Amauve C. du Rhône 2014	Red	€ 15.95	227
Ridge East Bench Zinfandel 2013, California	Red	€ 29.95	245
THE WICKLOW WINE COMPANY, MAIN STREET, WICKLOW			
Custoza 2014 Cantina di Custoza, Veneto	White	€ 12.95	29

STOCKISTS CONTINUED	Style	Price	Page No.
Terre d'Eglantier Réserve, Ardechois 2013	White	€ 16.95	101
Ka Manciné Rossesse di Dolceacqua 2014	Red	€ 26.00	155
Artuke Pies Negros 2013 Rioja	Red	€ 18.90	197
Dom Rafael 2012, Mouchâo, Alentejo	Red	€ 14.50	223
Casa Emma Chianti Classico Riserva 2010	Red	€ 39.95	249

WIDELY AVAILABLE
Frunza Pinot Noir 2014, Romania	Red	€ 9.99	121
Carmen Right Wave Pinot Noir 2014	Red	€ 14.99	135
Doña Paula Estate Malbec 2014, Uco Valley	Red	€ 15.99	229

THE WINE CENTRE, KILKENNY
Champagne Deutz Rosé NV	Sparkling	€ 65.00	19
Hunky Dory Sauvignon Blanc 2013	White	€ 18.99	43
Framingham Sauvignon Blanc 2014	White	€ 19.75	79
Pascual Toso Malbec 2013, Mendoza	White	€ 13.99	217
Jean Bousquet Cabernet Sauvignon 2013	Red	€ 15.50	225
Warre's Bottle-aged LBV Port 2003	Fortified	€ 35.00	255

THE WINE SHOP, PERRYSTOWN
Pegos Claros 2010, Palmela	Red	€ 14.99	185
Monte da Peceguina Red 2013	Red	€ 20.95	203

WINEONLINE.IE
Champagne Deutz Rosé NV Champagne	Sparkling	€ 65.00	19
Greywacke Wild Sauvignon Blanc 2013	White	€ 33.00	89

WINES DIRECT, MULINGAR WINESDIRECT.IE
Steininger Grüner Veltliner 2014, Kamptal	White	€ 15.80	59
Chardonnay Terres Dorées 2014 J-P. Brun	White	€ 18.95	73
Ch. Sainte-Marie Alios 2012 C. de Bordeaux	Red	€ 17.95	195

THEWINESHOP.IE
Ata Rangi Pinot Noir 2013, Martinborough	Red	€ 63.99	165

WINES ON THE GREEN & THE CELTIC WHISKEY SHOP, DAWSON ST
Veuve Cliquot Ponsardin Rosé 2004	Sparkling	€ 80.00	21
Tramin Pinot Grigio 2014	White	€ 15.99	61
Ribeo 2011, Morellino di Scansano	Red	€ 18.99	233
Barbeito 10 Year Old Reserve Sercial Madeira	Fortified	€ 37.99	257
Bodegas Tradición Palo Cortado VORS	Fortified	€ 84.99	261